100
essential
crochet
motifs

100 essential **crochet** motifs

Cassie Ward

Contents

Introduction	6
Materials and Tools	8
Basic Techniques	10
Stitches	11
Other Techniques	20
Finishing Off	22
Reading the Patterns	22
Key to charts	25
Traditional Granny Square	26
Solid Granny Square	27
Solid Half-and-half Square	28
Granny Half Square	29
Heart Square	30
Diamond in a Square	31
Little Granny Circle	32
Big Stitch Little Stitch	33
Daisy Daisy	34
Smiley Face	35
Circle Granny Square	36
Puff Stripe Square	37
Purple Haze	38
Stained-glass Window Square	39
Spiky Circle	40
Starburst Motif	41
Starflower Square	42
Raised Treble Square	43
Small Sunflower Square	44

Sherbet Surprise	45
African Violet Square	46
Mitred Flower	47
Snowflake Square	48
Half Rainbow	49
Sun Square	50
Moon Child	51
Twinkle Twinkle Little Star	52
Josie's Little Flower	53
Mixed Stitch Motif	54
Block By Block	55
Retro Flower Motif	56
Cluster Triangle Square	57
Carnation Square	58
Mini 3D Flower	59
Kaleidoscope Square	60
She Sells Seashells on the Sea Shore	61
Groovy Baby	62
Happy Flower	63
Bobbling Along Square	64
Gridlocked	65
In Full Bloom	66
Flower Chain Square	67
V-stitch Square	68
Spiral Swirl	69
Sidari Square	70
Alexis Square	71
Catherine Wheel	72

Little Pearl Square	73	Hexagon to Triangle	101
Orla Square	74	Flower in Mesh Triangle	102
Purple Twist	75	Cartwheel Triangle	103
Granny Hexagon	76	In a Whirl Triangle	104
Peaceful Hexagon	77	Triangle Flower	105
Daisy Hexagon	78	Openwork Triangle	106
Matisse Hexagon	79	Ivy's Triangle	107
African Violet Hexagon	80	Moss Stitch Triangle	108
Wagon Wheel Hexagon	81	Perfect Petal Triangle	109
Pretty Pink Hexagon	82	Heart Triangle	110
Starburst Hexagon	83	Solid Octagon	111
All the Blues Hexagon	84	Puff Stitch Octagon	112
Hexagon 3D Flower	85	Sophia Octagon	113
Circle in a Hexagon	86	Openwork Octagon	114
Moss Stitch Hexagon	87	African Violet Octagon	115
Nordic Hexagon	88	Blue Haze Octagon	116
Bobble Flower Hexagon	89	Puff Flower Octagon	117
Ribbed Hexagon	90	Chain-space Octagon	118
Seventies Hexagon Flower	91	Solid Pentagon	119
Star Hexagon	92	Granny Pentagon	120
Snowflake Hexagon	93	Peephole Pentagon	121
Scandi Hexagon	94	Pretty Flower Pentagon	122
Openwork Circle	95	Puff Stitch Pentagon	123
Solid Triangle	96	Ribbed Pentagon	124
Granny Triangle	97	African Violet Pentagon	125
African Violet-style Triangle	98		
Ribbed Triangle	99	Index	126
Circle in a Triangle	100	Acknowledgements	127

100 Essential Crochet Motifs

Introduction

Whether you're new to crochet or a seasoned crocheter, I hope this book will give you inspiration and enjoyment as you make these colourful motifs. For beginners, I've explained the basics of crochet and step-by-step instructions for all the stitches used in the book. Once you've mastered the art of holding the hook and yarn and taught yourself a few basic stitches, the crochet world is yours. And the wonderful thing about crochet is that once you've got the hang of it, you can create so many things with it.

About the motifs

The 100 crochet motifs in this book range in size, shape and complexity (see difficulty ratings, below) but are a fantastic starting point for your own creations. Join multiples of the same motif together to make a blanket, throw or cushion cover, or experiment with using the motifs in your own creations – a crochet square cardigan, or anything else you can think of.

For every motif, I've included a crochet chart, using the standard symbols for all the crochet stitches. I'd really recommend learning how to read a chart if you're interested in taking crochet further – it opens up a world of patterns to you, and you can even start to create your own designs.

Difficulty ratings

You will notice that I've colour coded the pages and added dot ratings. So pink pages and single dots are the easiest patterns, green pages with two green dots are a bit more challenging, and blue pages with three blue dots are the most complicated patterns. If you're starting out, start with one of the pink patterns, and even experienced crocheters might want to start with these to get a feel for how the patterns work. Once you're familiar with the stitches I've used, you can move on to the more complicated patterns. And... have fun!

100 Essential Crochet Motifs

Materials and Tools

The good thing about crochet as a hobby is that you really need very few tools. Once you've got a hook and your chosen yarn, you can begin. Here I've given you a guide to choosing your first hook and some useful tools you will need as you go further with crochet.

Yarn

I've chosen Scheepjes Catona yarn for all the motifs in this book. It comes in a fantastic range of colours – 113 of them no less – so you can create your projects in any shade you want.

It's made from 100% mercerised cotton, which makes it soft and easy to work with – as well as good for those with wool allergies. As it's a cotton yarn, Catona is also machine washable, although I'd recommend you hand-wash your crochet projects to avoid them stretching or going out of shape if your tension is a bit loose.

Catona is a 'fingering weight' yarn designed for crochet projects. It's a 4-ply yarn that is finer than other yarns you may be used to – double knit, for example – so select your hook size (see below) based on this to get the tension and size you want.

You can, of course, make these projects in any yarn you want. Feel free to go wild! Experiment with yarns and hook sizes to get the results you want.

Hooks

As with any new hobby you need the basic tools to begin with. There's a bewildering variety of crochet hooks, in different styles and made of different materials – metal, plastic, wood and even bamboo. There are hooks with straight handles and some with soft plastic handles that are comfortable but quite bulky to hold. Wooden and bamboo hooks are very light and nice to hold but they are quite expensive. Yet if you learn to crochet and fall in love with it like I did, it's well worth thinking about investing in some really nice hooks.

If you're new to crochet, I would recommend a metal hook to start with. Make sure it is smooth, undamaged, light and comfortable to hold. If the hook is damaged or rough it could catch on or split the yarn.

Hook size

I haven't specified a hook size for these motifs as it will depend on your preference and tension (see more on checking your tension on page 9).

For working with the Scheepjes Catona yarn I've recommended for these motifs, a hook between 2.5mm to 3.5mm is ideal. But if you're new to crochet, your first hook should be a reasonable size – 3.5mm or even 4mm – as it's easier to work with a larger hook.

If you're making the motifs with a different yarn, check the recommended hook size for the yarn – and experiment to see which size suits you best.

Useful tools

You will need scissors for trimming yarn and for when you're sewing up. Ideally, use a small pair of embroidery scissors so you don't run the risk of cutting into your project when you're trimming ends.

Use a yarn or embroidery needle to sew in yarn ends and for whip stitching your motifs together (see whip stitch on page 21). These needles have large eyes, so you can thread them with your yarn, and blunt points so that you don't damage your work when you are sewing in the ends.

If you want to join motifs together for a larger project, you'll need sewing pins for blocking out your motifs (see page 22) or for pinning them together to plan your finished project. Ideally, find long pins as they are easy to use. And you'll want a tape measure to check the motifs are the size you need.

Stitch markers

Stitch markers are very useful when working in the round, as it's sometimes difficult to see where a round ends and begins. They are plastic or metal clips that you can use to mark the beginning of each round so you don't lose track.

Yarn bobbin

Another helpful tool is a yarn bobbin. These are ideal for keeping your different coloured yarns tidy when you're working with a few colours in the same row. Otherwise, it can often be quite hard to stop the yarns tangling up. Yarn bobbins come in all sorts of shapes and sizes, but you can make your own yarn bobbins simply with pieces of card – the main thing is to wrap just the length of yarn you need around the bobbin, so you're not working with lots of bulky balls of yarn.

A soft bag

Find a soft cotton bag to keep your project clean and untangled when you're not working on it. Ideally, you'll want a bag that's large enough to keep your pattern book with your crochet, with separate pockets to keep the needles and scissors away from your crochet.

Tension

I haven't specified a recommended size or tension for these motifs as it will depend on the hook size and yarn you are using. If you're making single motifs, the finished size won't matter too much. If you're making these motifs into a larger project – such as a blanket, a cushion cover, or an item of clothing, for example – it is worth doing a test square to check the finished size of your motifs. This way you can adjust the hook size if the finished squares end up too big or too small for your project.

100 Essential Crochet Motifs

Basic Techniques

Once you've mastered a few basic techniques it is straightforward to start creating wonderful crochet projects. Get the hang of holding the hook and yarn so that you can work the stitches comfortably and you'll be off!

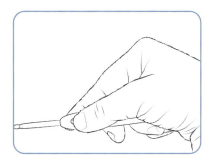

Holding the hook

Hold the hook in your dominant hand – so your right hand if you're right handed, your left hand if left handed (see 'tips for left-handers', below). Hold it comfortably so that you can easily manoeuvre the hook without it being awkward or too far away from your crochet.

The hook should be angled downwards, with the hook part facing towards you.

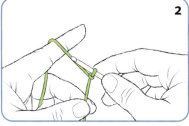

Holding the yarn

There's no one way to hold the yarn, it depends on what you find comfortable and what allows you to keep the right tension on the yarn as you work. Experiment with different ways of holding the yarn that allow you to keep some tension on the yarn without it being too tight for you to crochet easily, or so loose that your work loses its shape.

1 You can wrap the yarn over your little finger, then under the next two fingers and over your forefinger, or around your little finger then under and over your other fingers.

2 Use your thumb and middle finger to hold your crochet at the right tension and your forefinger to hold the yarn ready for the stitch.

Tips for left-handers

I am left-handed and I found it hard to learn how to crochet as all the people who had tried to teach me before were right-handed and I couldn't find a way to make it work for me. But don't despair – I am proof that it's possible to learn how to crochet left-handed and make a success of it!

The most important thing when crocheting with your left hand is to learn how to grip the hook and work the yarn to maintain the right tension in your stitches. Experiment with different grips for your hook and different ways of holding the yarn.

The stitch illustrations here show a right-handed crocheter, but if you're left-handed these patterns work just as well. Simply follow the patterns as usual, only as a left hander, you'll be working from left to right, or clockwise rather than anti-clockwise.

Another top tip is to learn how to read crochet charts. Once you can read a chart, you can easily make any project – the only difference is that you will be working from left to right rather than right to left around or along the chart.

Stitches

Here I've described the stitches I've used in these motifs. Start with the basic stitches to get familiar with the movement of the hook and don't forget that stitches are usually worked in both loops of the stitch below.

Slip knot

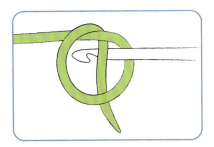

All your projects start with a simple slip knot. Make a loop with your yarn, insert the hook through the loop and pick up the ball end of the yarn, draw through loop and pull in tail end gently.

Yarn round hook (yrh)

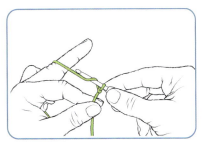

Wrap the yarn from back to front around your hook.

Chain (ch)

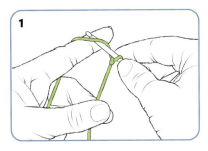
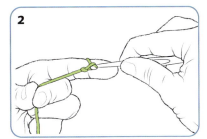

1 Start with a slip knot or loop on the hook and wrap the yarn round the hook (yrh).

2 Put the yarn through the loop on your hook.

3 To work more chain stitches, simply repeat the steps, so yarn round the hook, then pull the yarn through the loop.

Chain stitches at the beginning of a round or row are used to create a stitch of the right height for the round – so 3 chain stitches for a round of treble stitches and 2 chain stitches for a round of double crochet stitches.

Slip stitch (sl st)

Slip stitches are used to join rounds together, to join pieces together and to work along stitches or into chain spaces to get to the right place to start the next round or row.

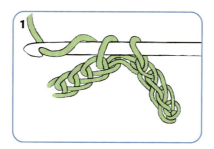 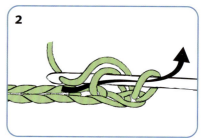

1 Insert your hook into the stitch or space indicated, wrap the yarn round your hook (yrh) and draw up a loop.

2 Pull this new loop through the loop on your hook to complete the stitch.

Chain spaces (ch-sp)

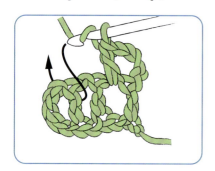

Chain stitches in a row or round will leave a gap in your crochet that you work into in the next round. So ch-sp is a 1-chain space, 2ch-sp is a 2-chain space etc.

When you're working into a chain space, you stitch around the chain rather than into the chain stitch itself.

Double crochet (dc)

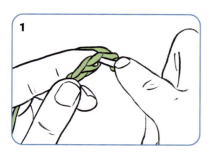 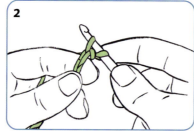 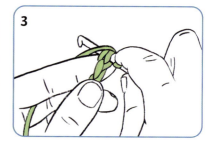

1 Insert hook into the top 2 loops of the stitch or into the chain space indicated.

2 Put the yarn round your hook (yrh) and draw up a loop through the stitch (2 loops on hook).

3 Wrap the yarn round your hook again and pull it through both loops on your hook to complete the stitch.

Treble (tr)

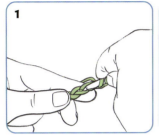 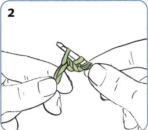 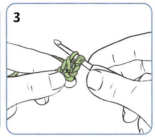 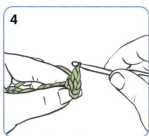

1 Wrap yarn round your hook (yrh) (2 loops on hook) then insert the hook into the stitch or space.

2 Wrap the yarn round the hook (yrh) again and pull it through the stitch (3 loops on hook).

3 Wrap the yarn round the hook (yrh) again and pull through 2 loops.

4 Wrap the yarn round the hook (yrh) again and pull through 2 loops to complete the stitch.

Half treble (htr)

 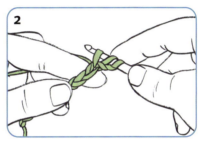 
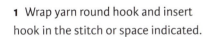

1 Wrap yarn round hook and insert hook in the stitch or space indicated.

2 Yarn round hook and draw yarn through the stitch (3 loops on hook).

3 Yarn round hook again and pull yarn through all 3 loops to complete the stitch.

Double treble (dtr)

 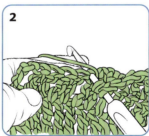 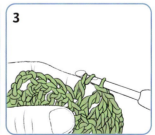 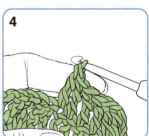

1 Wrap yarn twice round hook, and insert hook into stitch or space indicated.

2 Wrap the yarn round hook again and draw it through the stitch or space (4 loops on hook).

3 Wrap the yarn round hook (yrh) and draw through 2 loops. Yarn round hook and draw through 2 loops again.

4 Yarn round hook (yrh) and draw through 2 loops for the final time to complete the stitch.

Extended treble (etr)

1 Yarn round hook (yrh) and insert hook in the stitch or space indicated.

2 Yarn round hook and pull through the stitch or space (3 loops on hook).

3 Yarn round hook and draw through 1 loop only (3 loops on hook).

4 Yarn round hook and draw through 2 loops.

5 Yarn round hook and draw through 2 loops again to complete the stitch.

Treble 2 together (tr2tog)

Stitching together combines stitches together to decrease the number of stitches in the next row. It is also used to create a lovely pointed effect – see the Small Sunflower Square on page 44.

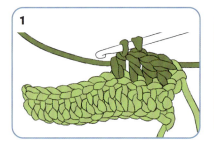
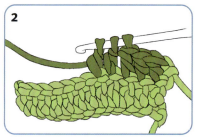
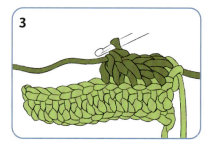

1 Working a treble as usual, yarn round hook (yrh), insert hook into stitch, yarn round hook again (yrn) and draw up a loop (3 loops on hook), then yarn round hook again and pull through 2 loops (2 loops on hook). Leave these loops and work the next treble.

2 Yarn round hook and insert hook into the next stitch, yarn round hook and draw through the stitch, yarn round hook and pull through 2 loops (3 loops on hook).

3 Finally, yarn round hook (yrh) and pull the yarn through all loops on the hook to finish both the trebles.

Treble 3 or more together (tr3tog)

You can treble multiple stitches together, just repeating step 1 above as many times as you need to get the required number of trebles. Finish the stitch by pulling through all the loops on your hook.

Triple treble (trtr)

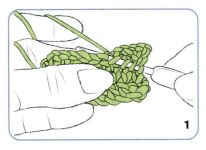
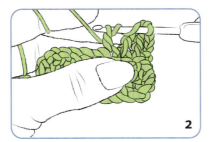

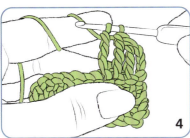

1 Yarn round hook 3 times and insert hook in stitch or space.

2 Yarn round hook and pull through 2 loops (4 loops on hook).

3 Yarn round hook and pull through 2 loops (3 loops on hook).

4 Yarn round hook and pull through 2 loops (2 loops on hook).

5 Yarn round hook and pull through both loops to complete stitch.

Work into one loop (blo and flo)

Stitches are usually worked into both loops of the stitch below. Working into the back or front loop only creates a ridge effect beneath the stitches on a row and can be used to shape the crochet by moving the stitches backwards or forwards from the previous row.

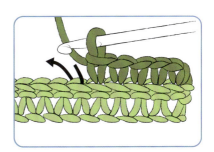

Back loop only (blo)
Insert hook into back part of stitch only (that is the back part of the 'V' looking down on the stitch from the top) then work the stitch as usual.

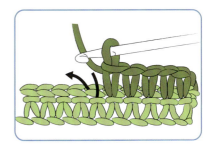

Front loop only (flo)
Insert hook into front part of the stitch only – the front part of the V looking down on the stitch from the top.

100 Essential Crochet Motifs

Cluster stitches (Cl)

Cluster stitches are worked in exactly the same way as treble or double treble togethers, but working into a single stitch.

Work each stitch as usual, leaving out the final step (yarn round hook and pull through final 2 loops). Then work the next stitch, again leaving out the final step. Repeat for the required number of stitches then do a final yarn round hook and pull through all the loops on your hook.

Variations in cluster stitches are shown using the stitch and number of stitches.

So, for example, a cluster of 3 treble stitches is a 3trCl and a cluster of 3 double treble stitches is a 3DdtrCl.

3 treble cluster (3trCl)

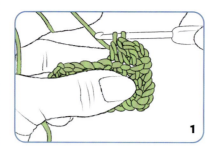 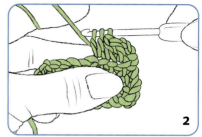

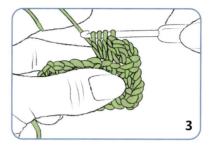 

1 Work a treble as usual, yarn round hook (yrh), insert hook into stitch, yarn round hook again (yrn) and draw up a loop (3 loops on hook), then yarn round hook again and pull through 2 loops (2 loops on hook). Leave these loops and work the next treble.

2 Work another treble as before into the same stitch or chain space. Do not pull through the final 2 loops of the treble (3 loops on hook). Leave these loops and work the next treble.

3 Work another treble as before into the same stitch or chain space. Do not pull through the final 2 loops of the treble (4 loops on hook).

4 Yarn round hook and draw yarn through all the loops on the hook to complete the cluster.

Beginning cluster (Beg Cl)

These stitches are identical to Cluster stitches, above, the only difference is the beginning chain stitches to get the round or row to the height of the first stitch.

So, for example, a beginning double treble cluster (Beg3dtrCl) starts with 4 chain stitches; a beginning treble cluster (Beg2trCl) starts with 3 chain stitches.

Popcorn (pop)

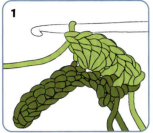 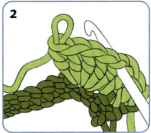 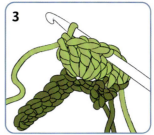 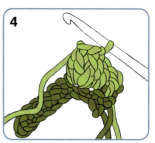

1 Work 5 trebles in stitch or chain space as indicated.

2 Remove hook from loop on last stitch and insert it under the loops of the first treble from front to back.

3 Catch loop of fifth treble and pull it through the loops of the first treble.

4 Pull the loop through to close with the 5 treble stitches in front.

Beginning popcorn (BegPop)

Beginning popcorn stitch is exactly the same as a popcorn stitch but starts with 3 chain stitches at the beginning and then 4 trebles instead of 5 trebles.

Puff stitch (puff)

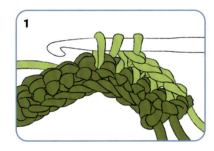 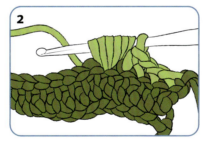 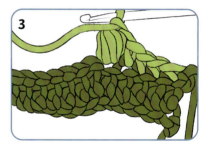

1 Yarn round hook, insert hook in stitch or space indicated, yarn round hook again and pull up a loop to height of 1 treble stitch.

2 Repeat step 1 twice more in the same stitch or space (7 loops on hook).

3 Yarn round hook and pull through all 7 loops, 1 chain stitch to complete the stitch.

Beginning puff stitch (BegPuff)

Beginning puff stitch is identical to puff stitch, but the 3 chain at the beginning replaces 2 of the loops, so in step 2 you repeat step 1 only once to have 5 loops on the hook.

100 Essential Crochet Motifs

Front post treble crochet (fptc)

This stitch is worked in the 'post' of the next stitch – the vertical part of the stitch below the top V of the stitch.

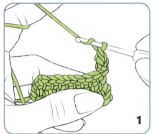 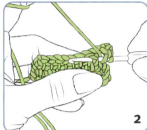 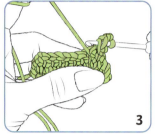 

1 Yarn round hook.

2 Insert the hook from front to back to front again around the vertical post of the next stitch.

3 Yarn round hook again and draw through the post (3 loops on hook).

4 Yarn round hook and draw through 2 loops. Yarn round hook and draw through remaining 2 loops to complete the stitch.

Raised triple treble front (rtrtrf)

This is a variation of front post treble crochet, worked in exactly the same way, except that the finished stitch is a triple treble instead of a treble stitch.

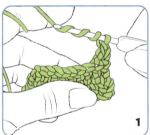 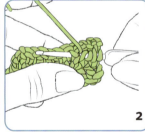  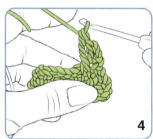

1 Yarn round hook 3 times.

2 Insert hook around the post of the next stitch from front to back to front.

3 Yarn round hook and pull up yarn around the post (5 loops on hook.

4 Yarn round hook and pull through 2 loops, 4 times.

Shells

Shells or groups are formed by working the given number of stitches into the same stitch or chain space to create a shell or fan effect.

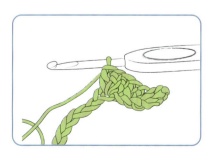

18   100 Essential Crochet Motifs

Back post treble crochet (bptc)

Worked in the same way as front post treble crochet, but this time working from back to front to back around the vertical post of the next stitch.

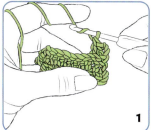  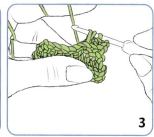 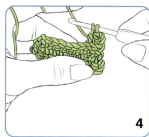

1 Yarn round hook.

2 Insert hook from back to front to back around vertical post of next stitch.

3 Yarn round hook and draw up the yarn through the stitch (3 loops on hook).

4 Yarn round hook and draw through 2 loops. Yarn round hook and draw through remaining 2 loops to complete the stitch.

Spike stitches

Spike stitches work into the row or round below the one you are working into. The stitches are then completed in the usual way.

Spike double crochet (Sp-dc)

Insert hook into the row or designated stitch below the round you are working into, yarn round hook and draw up yarn to the height of the current row, yarn round hook again and draw yarn through both loops to complete the double crochet.

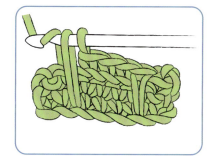

Spike treble (Sp-tr)

Yarn round hook, insert hook in row or stitch indicated below the round or row you are working into, yarn round hook again and draw up yarn to the height of the current row, yarn round hook again and pull through 2 loops, yarn round hook again and pull through 2 loops to complete the stitch.

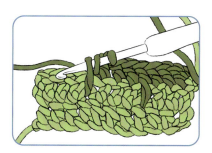

Bobble

Bobble stitches are 6 unfinished treble stitches worked into the same stitch then closed off at the end to create a bobble effect.

1 Yarn round hook twice, insert hook into stitch and pull yarn through stitch. Yarn round hook, pull through 2 loops. Yarn round hook, pull through 2 loops. Repeat these steps 5 times until you have 6 loops on the hook.

2 Yarn round hook again and pull yarn through all 6 loops to complete the bobble stitch.

Other Techniques

Once you've mastered the stitches, you are most of the way to being a crocheter. Here we cover how to change colours, read the crochet patterns, work with crochet charts and how to finish off your projects.

Joining a new colour

For most of the projects, joining in a new colour is quite straightforward – you're often fastening off one strand of yarn and joining in another.

If you're joining a new colour into a chain space, you can simply tie the yarn around the chain space to join, leaving a long enough end to sew in later.

Otherwise, you can join in the new colour using a slip stitch.

Joining in a round

When joining in a new colour in the middle of a row or round, work the last step of the stitch in the new colour. Catch the yarn in the new colour and draw through the loops on the hook to complete the stitch.

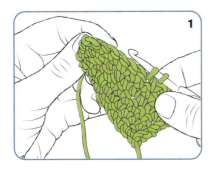 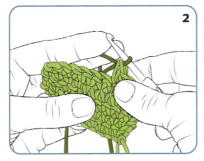 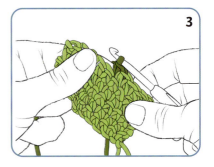

1 Work the final stitch of yarn A, leaving the final 2 loops on your hook.

2 Join in yarn B and complete the final stitch of yarn A with the new colour.

3 Continue to work stitches in yarn B.

20   100 Essential Crochet Motifs

Managing your yarn colours

For the half and half squares, be careful to keep the yarns separate as you want to drop them then pick them up again when you need them.

When you're changing colours in a row or round and need to carry colours over, you can hide it on the wrong side of your crochet by working over the yarn strand every few stitches.

For crochet projects where both sides will be visible and you need to carry yarn colours across the work, just work over the yarn you're not using with every stitch, covering it with the new colour. You won't need to use this technique in these motifs!

Fastening off

To fasten off at the end of your project, cut the yarn (leaving enough to sew in the ends), then pull the yarn through the final stitch until it is fully closed.

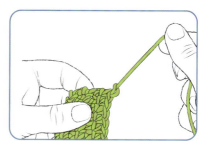

Sewing in ends

To finish off your work, you'll need to sew in all the yarn ends. Thread an embroidery needle with the yarn end, and work it into stitches of the same colour, first going one way then back the other way. Then snip off the remaining end as close as possible to your work.

Joining motifs

To join your motifs together or to join mini-motifs without crocheting them together, I use whip stitch.

First, make sure the two pieces are pinned against each other in the location the pattern states. Thread a large embroidery needle with the leftover tail of the first piece being attached and insert the needle under the stitch of the matched-up stitch on the second piece and pull it through. Next, bring the needle back up and under both loops of the next stitch on the piece that is being attached and pull it tight. Then insert the needle under the next stitch of the second piece. Repeat the steps until both pieces are secure.

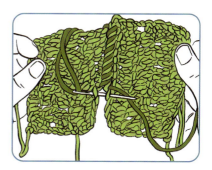

Finishing off

Once you've sewn in your ends, you'll want to make sure your motifs look as perfect as possible. If you're joining lots of the same motifs together into a larger project, like a blanket, you may want to sew them together without blocking. But if you're using motifs of different shapes, and need them to fit perfectly together, I'd recommend you block all your individual motifs first.

Blocking

First, lightly moisten your project. You can either do this by laying it out onto a towel then giving it a quick spray with a water spritzer, or by using an iron to steam it gently – don't press down, just use the steam to moisten it. The yarn I've used here is cotton, so can be pressed directly if you prefer. But for other yarns with acrylic mixes, a hot iron will melt the yarn and ruin your project! Then you can use long sewing pins, or blocking pins, to fix your motif into shape. You can do this either on a special blocking board, or just use a piece of corrugated card or foam. As the motif dries out, the pins will ensure it dries into the right shape.

Alternatively, you can pin out your project first, then steam it and leave it to dry into shape. Experiment with which of these methods you prefer.

Reading the patterns

If you are new to crochet, it may take you some time to get used to the way crochet patterns are written. In particular, you'll want to become familiar with the stitch abbreviations so you don't have to flip back and forth all the time! Once you've got used to the way the patterns are written, you will find these motifs easy to follow. Start with the easier patterns and take it from there. US readers, please note that I've used UK stitches and abbreviations throughout – check the chart opposite for their US equivalents.

Pattern repeats

In most crochet patterns, stitches are repeated in a row or round. To indicate this, I've used * to show you where to repeat from and how many times to repeat the stitches. For the longer patterns with lots of repeats, I've put some of the instructions in square brackets [ ] and told you how many times in total to do the stitches in the [ ].

Crochet charts

For each pattern, I've included a crochet chart, using symbols for each stitch or instruction. You read from the inside out – or from the bottom up if you're reading patterns in rows rather than rounds. Right-handed crocheters go anti-clockwise round a chart. If you're left-handed, follow the chart clockwise.

For rounds where you have turned the work, you still work in the same direction – even though you are working back along the stitches you've just done in the previous round.

In each round, the start of the round is marked with a dot. It's also fairly easy to work out the beginning of a round as almost all rounds start with chain stitches. Then, using the stitch chart, you can simply work each round, stitch by stitch, following the chart until you've reached the end of the round.

In these charts, we've used the colours of the yarn for each round to make it even easier to follow. You'll notice that the symbols don't specify whether you're working into a stitch or a chain space. In most cases, this is easy to work out, but of course you can also refer back to the pattern to double check.

If you want to become proficient in reading charts, start by copying and printing out the chart of the motif you're working on (bigger if possible). Then you can mark stitch-by-stitch as you work around the chart. It's well worth persevering with learning to read the charts as, once you get the hang of it, crochet charts can open up a whole new world of crochet patterns to you!

Crochet terms

UK crochet terms
Double crochet
Half treble
Treble
Double treble
Triple treble
Extended treble

US crochet terms
Single crochet
Half double crochet
Double crochet
Triple crochet
Double triple crochet
Extended double crochet

Abbreviations

blo	back loop only	htr	half treble
BegCl	beginning cluster	pop	popcorn stitch
BegPop	beginning pop stitch	puff	puff stitch
BegPuff	beginning puff stitch	rep	repeat
bobble	bobble stitch	rtrtrf	raised triple treble front post
bptr	back post treble crochet	RS	right side
ch	chain	sl st	slip stitch
ch-loop	chain loop	sp	space
ch-sp	chain space	Sp-dc	Spike double crochet
2ch-sp	2-chain space (etc.)	Sp-tr	Spike treble crochet
Cl	cluster	tr	treble crochet
dc	double crochet	trCl	treble cluster
dtr	double treble	trtr	triple treble
dtrCl	double treble cluster	tr2tog	treble 2 together
etr	extended treble	v-stitch	V-stitch (tr, ch, tr)
flo	front loop only	WS	wrong side
fptr	front post treble crochet	yrh	yarn round hook

100 Essential Crochet Motifs

Key to charts

- ⬭ Chain
- ● Slip Stitch
- ✝ Double Crochet
- ⊤ Half Treble Crochet
- ƒ Treble Crochet
- ƒ Double Treble Crochet
- ƒ Triple Treble Crochet
- Λ Treble Decrease
- Λ Double Treble Decrease (dtr3tog)
- Extended Treble Crochet
- Raised Triple Treble Front
- ⌒ Back Loop Only
- Puff Stitch
- 2-Treble Cluster (tr2Cl)
- 3-Treble Cluster (3trCl)
- 3-Double Treble Cluster (dtr3Cl)

- 4-Treble Cluster (4trCl)
- Popcorn Stitch
- Bobble Stitch
- V-Stitch
- Treble 2 Together (tr2tog)
- Double Treble 2 Together (dtr2tog)
- Treble 3 Together (tr3tog)
- DoubleTreble 3 Together (dtr3tog)
- Treble 4 Together (tr4tog)
- Treble 5 Together (tr5tog)
- Treble 6 Together (tr6tog)
- Front Post Treble Crochet
- Back Post Treble Crochet
- Spike Double Crochet
- Spike Treble Crochet

Motif 1:
Traditional Granny Square

This traditional granny square is finished with a round of double crochet edging.

Yarn A
208 Yellow Gold

Yarn B
114 Shocking Pink

Yarn C
222 Tulip

Yarn D
189 Royal Orange

Yarn E
386 Peach

Yarn F
130 Old Lace

Turn after each round.
Using yarn A, 4 ch, sl st to first ch to form a ring.
Round 1: 3 ch (counts as 1 tr throughout), 2 tr in ring, 2 ch, (3 tr, 2 ch) 3 times in ring, join with sl st to top of 3 ch. Fasten off.
Change to yarn B.
Round 2: 3 ch, (2 tr, 2 ch, 3 tr) in same 2ch-sp, (3 tr, 2 ch, 3 tr) in each 2ch-sp, sl st to join.
Change to yarn C.
Round 3: 3 ch, 2 tr in sp between 3 tr groups, (3 tr, 2 ch, 3 tr) in next 2ch-sp, *3 tr in next sp, (3 tr, 2 ch, 3 tr) in next 2ch-sp; rep from * twice more, sl st to top of 3 ch.
Change to yarn D.
Round 4: 3 ch, 2 tr in sp between 3 tr groups, (3 tr, 2 ch, 3 tr) in next 2ch-sp, *3 tr in each 2ch-sp to next corner 2ch-sp, (3 tr, 2 ch, 3 tr) in corner 2ch-sp; rep from * twice more, 3 tr in next sp, sl st to top of 3 ch.
Change to yarn E.
Round 5: 3 ch, 2 tr in same sp, (3 tr, 2 ch, 3 tr) in next 2ch-sp, *3 tr in each 2ch-sp to next corner 2ch-sp, (3 tr, 2 ch, 3 tr) in corner 2ch-sp; rep from * twice more, 3 tr in each sp to end, sl st to top of 3 ch.
Change to yarn F.
Round 6: As round 5.
Round 7: *1 dc in each tr to corner, (1 dc, 2 ch, 1 dc) in corner; rep from * 3 times, 1 dc in remaining tr sts, sl st to join. Fasten off.

100 Essential Crochet Motifs

Motif 2:
Solid Granny Square

Using rounds of treble stitches gives this granny square a more delicate appearance.

Yarn A 🟥
256 Cornelia Rose

Yarn D 🟦
511 Cornflower

Yarn B 🟩
389 Apple Green

Yarn E 🟨
208 Yellow Gold

Yarn C 🟦
384 Powder Blue

Yarn F ⬜
130 Old Lace

Using yarn A, 4 ch, sl st to form a ring.

Round 1: 3 ch (counts as 1 tr throughout), 2 tr in ring, 2 ch, (3 tr, 2 ch) 3 times in ring, sl st to top of 3 ch, turn. Fasten off A. Join yarn B in any 2ch-sp.

Round 2: (3 ch, 1 tr, 2 ch, 2 tr) in 2ch-sp, 3 tr, [(2 tr, 2 ch, 2 tr) in next 2ch-sp, 3 tr] 3 times, sl st to top of 3 ch, turn. Fasten off B. Join yarn C in any corner 2ch-sp.

Round 3: (3 ch, 1 tr, 2 ch, 2 tr) in 2ch-sp, 7 tr, [(2 tr, 2 ch, 2 tr) in corner 2ch-sp, 7 tr] 3 times, sl st to top of 3 ch, turn. Fasten off C. Join yarn D in any corner 2ch-sp.

Round 4: (3 ch, 1 tr, 2 ch, 2 tr) in 2ch-sp, 11 tr, [(2 tr, 2 ch, 2 tr) in next 2ch-sp, 11 tr] 3 times, sl st to top of 3 ch, turn. Fasten off D. Join yarn E in any corner 2ch-sp.

Round 5: (3 ch, 1 tr, 2 ch, 2 tr) in 2ch-sp, 1 tr in each tr to corner space, [(2 tr, 2 ch, 2 tr) in next 2ch-sp, 1 tr in each tr to corner 2ch-sp] 3 times, sl st to top of 3 ch. Fasten off E. Join yarn F in any corner 2ch-sp.

Round 6: Rep round 5.

Round 7: [1 dc in each tr to corner 2ch-sp, (1 dc, 2 ch, 1 dc) in corner 2ch-sp] 4 times, 1 dc in remaining tr sts, sl st to join. Fasten off.

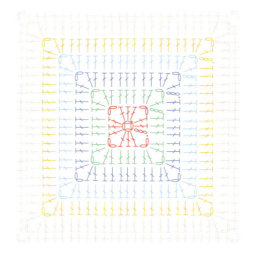

Motif 3:
Solid Half-and-half Square

Join several of these squares together to make a lovely geometrical design for a larger project.

Yarn A
130 Old Lace

Yarn B
280 Lemon

Turn after each round.

Using yarn A, 4 ch, sl st to first st to form a ring.

Round 1: 3 ch (counts as 1 tr), (2 tr, 2 ch, 3 tr) in ring, 1 ch, Join in yarn B (do not fasten off yarn A): 1 ch, (3 tr, 2 ch, 3 tr), 2 ch, sl st to join.

Round 2: Sl st in corner 2ch-sp, 3 ch, 1 tr in same corner 2ch-sp, 3 tr, (2 tr, 2 ch, 2 tr) in next corner 2ch-sp, 3 tr, 2 tr in next corner 2ch-sp, 1 ch.

Pick up yarn A: 1 ch, 2 tr in same corner 2ch-sp, 3 tr, (2 tr, 2 ch, 2 tr) in next corner 2ch-sp, 3 tr, 2 tr in first corner 2ch-sp, 2 ch, sl st in 3rd of beg 3 ch to join.

Round 3: Sl st in corner 2ch-sp, 3 ch, 1 tr in same corner 2ch-sp, 1 tr in each tr to next corner 2ch-sp, (2 tr, 2 ch, 2 tr) in 2ch-sp, 1 tr in each tr to next corner 2ch-sp, 2 tr in 2ch-sp, 1 ch.

Pick up yarn B: 1 ch, 2 tr in same 2ch-sp, 1 tr in each tr to next corner 2ch-sp, (2 tr, 2 ch, 2 tr) in 2ch-sp, 1 tr in each tr to original 2ch-sp, 2 tr in 2ch-sp, 2 ch, sl st in 3rd of beg 3 ch to join.

Round 4: Sl st in corner 2ch-sp, 3 ch, 1 tr in same 2ch-sp, 1 tr in each tr to next corner 2ch-sp, (2 tr, 2 ch, 2 tr) in 2ch-sp, 1 tr in each tr to next corner 2ch-sp, 2 tr in 2ch-sp, 1 ch.

Pick up yarn A: 1 ch, 2 tr in same 2ch-sp, 1 tr in each tr to next corner 2ch-sp, (2 tr, 2 ch, 2 tr) in 2ch-sp, 1 tr in each tr to original 2ch-sp, 2 tr in 2ch-sp, 2 ch, sl st in 3rd of beg 3 ch to join.

Round 5: As round 3. Fasten off.

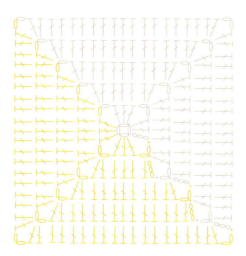

Notes
For these half-and-half squares, don't work over the other yarn, but drop each colour ready to pick up again on the next round. This technique gives you a clean line between the different yarn colours.

Motif 4:
Granny Half Square

This variation on the traditional granny square creates a shell-like effect with the groups of trebles.

Yarn A
130 Old Lace

Yarn B
222 Tulip

Turn after each round.
Using yarn A, 4 ch, sl st to first ch to form a ring.
Round 1: 3 ch (counts as 1 tr), (2 tr, 2 ch, 3 tr) in ring, 1 ch, join in yarn B (do not fasten off yarn A): 1 ch, (3 tr, 2 ch, 3 tr) all in ring, 2 ch, sl st in 3rd of beg 3 ch.
Round 2: Sl st in corner 2ch-sp, 3 ch, 2 tr in corner 2ch-sp, (3 tr, 2 ch, 3 tr) in next corner 2ch-sp, 3 tr in next corner 2ch-sp, 1 ch.
Pick up yarn A: 1 ch, 3 tr in same corner 2ch-sp, (3 tr, 2 ch, 3 tr) in next corner 2ch-sp, 3 tr in first corner 2ch-sp, 2 ch, sl st in 3rd of beg 3 ch.
Round 3: Sl st in corner 2ch-sp, (3 ch, 2 tr) in same 2ch-sp, 3 tr in space between 3 tr groups, (3 tr, 2 ch, 3 tr) in next corner 2ch-sp, 3 tr in space between 3 tr groups, 3 tr in next corner 2ch-sp, 1 ch.
Pick up yarn B: 1 ch, 3 tr in same corner 2ch-sp, 3 tr in space between 3 tr groups, (3 tr, 2 ch, 3 tr) in next corner 2ch-sp, 3 tr in space between 3 tr groups, 3 tr in first corner 2ch-sp, 2 ch, sl st in 3rd of beg 3 ch.
Round 4: Sl st in corner 2ch-sp, (3 ch, 2 tr) in same 2ch-sp, 3 tr in space between each 3 tr group to corner, (3 tr, 2 ch, 3 tr) in 2ch-sp, 3 tr in space between each 3 tr group to corner, 3 tr in 2ch-sp, 1 ch.
Pick up yarn A: 1 ch, 3 tr in same corner 2ch-sp, 3 tr in space between 3 tr groups to corner, (3 tr, 2 ch, 3 tr) in 2ch-sp, 3 tr in space between 3 tr groups to first corner, 3 tr in 2ch-sp, 2 ch, sl st in 3rd of beg 3 ch.
Round 5: Sl st in corner 2ch-sp, (3 ch, 2 tr) in same 2ch-sp, 3 tr in space between each 3 tr group to corner, (3 tr, 2 ch, 3 tr) in 2ch-sp, 3 tr in space between each 3 tr group to corner, 3 tr in 2ch-sp, 1 ch.
Pick up yarn B: 1 ch, 3 tr in same corner 2ch-sp, 3 tr in space between 3 tr groups to corner, (3 tr, 2 ch, 3 tr) in 2ch-sp, 3 tr in space between 3 tr groups to first corner, 3 tr in 2ch-sp, 2 ch, sl st in 3rd of beg 3 ch.

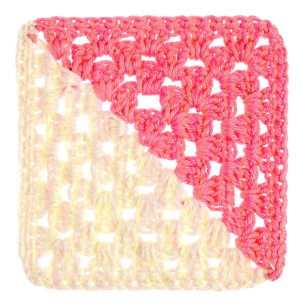

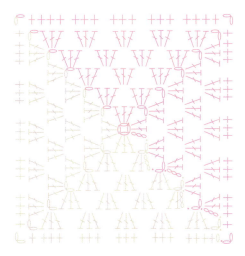

Round 6: Sl st in corner 2ch-sp, 1 ch, 1 dc in same 2ch-sp, 1 dc in each tr to next corner 2ch-sp, (1 dc, 2 ch, 1 dc) in corner 2ch-sp, 1 dc in each tr to next corner 2ch-sp, 1 dc in corner 2ch-sp, 1 ch.
Pick up yarn A: 1 ch, 1 dc in same corner 2ch-sp, 1 dc in each tr to next corner 2ch-sp, (1 dc, 2 ch, 1 dc) in corner 2ch-sp, 1 dc in each st to first corner sp, sl st in first ch. Fasten off.

100 Essential Crochet Motifs

Motif 5:
Heart Square

For this vibrant square, cut and rejoin yarn shades as you go, leaving lengths to darn in ends.

Yarn A
222 Tulip

Yarn B
189 Royal Orange

Turn after each round.
Using yarn A, 4 ch, sl st to join.

Round 1: 3 ch (counts as 1 tr), 2 tr in ring, 2 ch, (3 tr, 2 ch) 3 times in ring, sl st to top of beg 3 ch to join.

Round 2: Sl st to first 2ch-sp, (3 ch, 2 tr, 2 ch, 3 tr) in same 2ch-sp, (3 tr, 2 ch, 3 tr) in each corner 2ch-sp around, sl st to top of beg 3 ch to join.

Round 3: Sl st to first corner 2ch-sp, (3 ch, 2 tr, 2 ch, 3 tr) in same 2ch-sp, 3 tr in space before next 3 tr group.
Join in yarn B on last pull through of last st, (cut yarn A): (3 tr, 2 ch, 3 tr) in corner 2ch-sp.
Join in yarn A in last loop of last tr: 3 tr in space before next 3 tr, (cut yarn A).
Join in yarn B in last loop of final tr: (3 tr, 2 ch, 3 tr) in corner 2ch-sp.
Join in yarn A in loop of last tr: 3 tr in space before next 3 tr, (3 tr, 2 ch, 3 tr) in corner 2ch-sp, (do not cut yarn A).
Join in yarn B: 3 tr in space before next 3 tr, sl st to join.

Round 4: With yarn B: 3 ch, 2 tr in same space, 3 tr in next space, (cut yarn B).
With yarn A: (3 tr, 2 ch, 3 tr) in corner sp, 3 tr in next sp.
With yarn B: 3 tr in next sp, (3 tr, 2 ch, 3 tr) in corner sp, 3 tr in next 2 sps, (3 tr, 2 ch, 3 tr) in corner sp, 3 tr in next sp.
With yarn A: 3 tr in next sp, (3 tr, 2 ch, 3 tr) in final corner sp, sl st to join.

Round 5: Join yarn B in any corner 2ch-sp, (3 ch, 2 tr, 2 ch, 3 tr) in corner, 3 tr in sp between each 3 tr group to next corner, *(3 tr, 2 ch, 3 tr) in corner sp, 3 tr in sp between each 3 tr group to next corner; rep from * twice more, sl st to join.

Round 6: *1 dc in each tr to corner, (1 dc, 2 ch, 1 dc) in corner; rep from * 3 times, 1 dc in remaining tr sts, sl st to join. Fasten off.

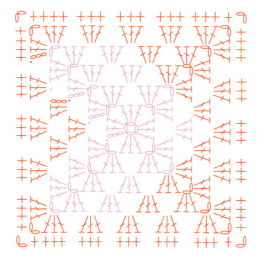

Motif 6:
Diamond in a Square

Ever wondered how to get a square to look like a diamond? This gorgeous motif is how.

Yarn A
386 Peach

Yarn B
522 Primrose

Yarn C
519 Freesia

Yarn D
511 Cornflower

Yarn E
509 Baby Blue

Using yarn A, ch 4, sl st to first ch to form a ring.
Round 1: 3 ch (counts as 1 tr) 2 tr in ring, 2 ch, (3 tr, 2 ch) 3 times in ring, sl st to top of 3 ch, turn.
Change to yarn B.
Round 2: 3 ch, (2 tr, 2 ch, 3 tr) in same 2ch-sp, (3 tr, 2 ch, 3 tr) in each 2ch-sp, sl st to join, turn.
Change to yarn C.
Round 3: 3 ch, 2 tr in sp between 3 tr groups, (3 tr, 2 ch, 3 tr) in next 2ch-sp, *3 tr in next sp, (3 tr, 2 ch, 3 tr) in next 2ch-sp; rep from * twice more, sl st to top of 3 ch, turn.
Change to yarn D.
Round 4: 3 ch, 2 tr in sp between 3 tr groups, (3 tr, 2 ch, 3 tr) in next 2ch-sp, *3 tr in each sp to next corner 2ch-sp, (3 tr, 2 ch, 3 tr) in 2ch-sp; rep from * twice more, 3 tr in next sp, sl st to top of 3 ch, turn.
Change to yarn E.

Corners

Repeat on each of the 4 corner sides.
Row 1: Join yarn E in one of the 4 corner 2ch-sp working only to the next corner 2ch-sp work as follows, 3 ch, miss 3 tr, 3 tr in each of next 3 spaces between trs, miss 3 tr, 1 tr in corner space, turn.
Row 2: 3 ch, miss 3 tr, 3 tr in next 2 spaces between trs, miss 3 tr, 1 tr in top of first tr from row 1.
Row 3: 3 ch, miss 3 tr, 3 tr in space between trs, miss 3 tr, 1 tr in top of first tr from row 2.
Row 4: 3 ch, 1 tr in first tr from row 3. Fasten off.

Once all 4 corners have been completed, rejoin yarn E in any corner space (formed by 3 ch and 1 tr in row 4).
Round 1: *(2 dc, 2 ch, 2 dc) in corner, 2 dc in each side of tr to corner of original diamond, 1 dc in that corner, 2 dc in each side of tr to corner; rep from * 3 times, sl st to join. Fasten off.

100 Essential Crochet Motifs

Motif 7:
Little Granny Circle

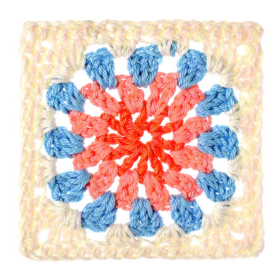

The combination of treble and half-treble stitches turns this circle into a square.

Yarn A
256 Cornelia Rose

Yarn C
384 Powder Blue

Yarn B
222 Tulip

Yarn D
130 Old Lace

Turn after each round.
Using yarn A, 4 ch, sl st to first ch to form a ring.
Round 1: 4 ch (counts as 1 tr, 1 ch), (1 tr, 1 ch) 11 times in ring, sl st to top of beg 3 ch to join. Fasten off.
Join yarn B in any ch-sp.
Round 2: 3 ch (counts as first tr), 1 tr in same ch-sp, 1 ch, (2 tr, 1 ch) in each ch-sp around, sl st to join. Fasten off.
Join yarn C in any 1 ch-sp.
Round 3: 3 ch, 2 tr in same ch-sp, 1 ch, (3 tr, 1 ch) in each ch-sp around, sl st to join. Fasten off.
Join yarn D in any ch-sp.
Round 4: 3 ch, (2 tr, 2 ch, 3 tr) in same ch-sp, 3 htr in next two 1 ch-sps, *(3 tr, 2 ch, 3 tr) in next ch-sp, 3 htr in next two 1 ch-sps; rep from * twice more, sl st to join.
Round 5: * 1 dc in each dc to corner space, (1 dc, 2 ch 1 dc) in corner space; rep from * 3 times, 1 dc in each dc, sl st to join. Fasten off.

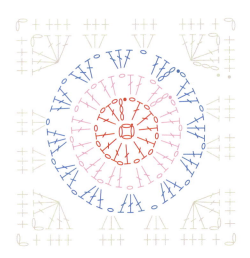

Motif 8:
Big Stitch Little Stitch

This motif looks complicated, but the dotty effect is created by repeating two simple rows.

Yarn A
397 Cyan

Yarn B
100 Lemon Chiffon

Yarn C
146 Vivid Blue

Yarn D
264 Light Coral

Yarn E
522 Primrose

Turn after each round.
Using yarn A, 4 ch, sl st to first st to form a ring.
Round 1: 3 ch (counts as 1 tr), (2 tr, 2 ch) into ring, *(3 tr, 2 ch) into ring; rep from * twice more, sl st to join.
Round 2: Join yarn B to 2ch-sp, (1 dc, 3 ch, 1 dc, 3 ch) in each corner space, sl st to join in top of first dc.
Round 3: Join yarn C in any corner 3ch-sp, 3 ch, (2 tr, 2 ch, 3 tr) in same corner space, 3 tr in 3ch-sp, *(3 tr, 2 ch, 3 tr) in corner space, 3 tr in 3ch-sp; rep from * twice more, sl st to join.
Round 4: Join Yarn B to corner space, *(1 dc, 3 ch, 1 dc) in corner space, (3 ch, miss 3 tr, 1 dc between last 3 tr group and next 3 tr group) twice, 3 ch, miss 3 tr; rep from * 3 times, sl st to first dc.
Round 5: Join Yarn D in any corner 3ch-sp, 3 ch, (2 tr, 2 ch, 3 tr) in same corner space, 3 tr in each 3ch-sp to corner, *(3 tr, 2 ch, 3 tr) in corner space, 3 tr in each 3ch-sp to corner; rep from * twice more, sl st to join.
Round 6: Join Yarn B to corner space, *(1 dc, 3 ch, 1 dc) in corner space, (3 ch, miss 3 tr, 1 dc between last 3 tr group and next 3 tr group) 3 times, 3 ch miss 3 tr; rep from * 3 times, sl st to first dc.
Round 7: Join Yarn E in any corner 3ch-sp, 3 ch, (2 tr, 2 ch, 3 tr) in same corner space, 3 tr in each 3ch-sp to corner, *(3 tr, 2 ch, 3 tr) in corner space, 3 tr in each 3ch-sp to corner; rep from * twice more, sl st to join.
Round 8: Join Yarn B to corner space, *(1 dc, 3 ch, 1 dc) in corner space, (3 ch, miss 3 tr, 1 dc between last 3 tr group and next 3 tr group) 4 times, 3 ch, miss 3 tr; rep from * 3 times, sl st to first dc.

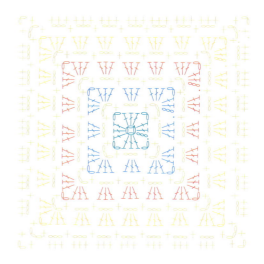

Round 9: Sl st into corner space, *(1 dc, 2 ch, 1 dc) in corner space, 3 dc in each 3ch-sp to corner; rep from * 3 times, sl st to join. Fasten off.

Motif 9:
Daisy Daisy

Use these beautiful daisy squares to make a gorgeous blanket or cushion for a really summery feel.

Yarn A
208 Yellow Gold

Yarn C
514 Jade

Yarn B
130 Old Lace

Turn after each round.
Using yarn A, 4 ch, sl st to form a ring.
Round 1: 3 ch (counts as 1 tr here and throughout), 11 tr in ring, sl st to top of 3 ch to join. Fasten off.
Join yarn B in top of any tr.
Round 2: 1 BegPuff, 2 ch, (1 puff in next tr, 2 ch) around, sl st to top of 3 ch of BegPuff. Fasten off.
Join yarn C in any 2ch-sp.
Round 3: 3 ch, (2 tr, 2 ch, 3 tr) in same 2ch-sp, 3 tr in each of next two 2ch-sps, *(3 tr, 2 ch, 3 tr) in next 2ch-sp, 3 tr in each of next two 2ch-sps; rep from * twice more, sl st to top of 3 ch to join.
Round 4: Sl st to any corner 2ch-sp, (3 ch, 2 tr, 2 ch, 3 tr) in same 2ch-sp, 3 tr in each space between 3 tr groups to corner space, *(3 tr, 2 ch, 3 tr) in corner 2ch-sp, 3 tr in each space between 3 tr groups to corner; rep from * twice more, sl st to join.
Round 5: *1 dc in each tr to corner, (1 dc, 2 ch, 1 dc); rep from * 3 times, 1 dc in remaining tr sts, sl st to join. Fasten off.

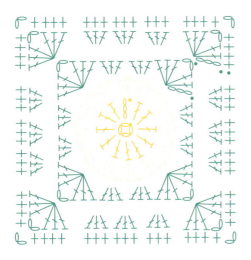

Notes
This motif uses beginning puff (BegPuff) and puff stitches. For instructions, see page 17.

Motif 10:
Smiley Face

This motif can't help but put a smile on your face. Embroider different expressions to mix it up a bit.

Yarn A
280 Lemon

Yarn C
110 Jet Black

Yarn B
114 Shocking Pink

Using yarn A, 4 ch, sl st to form a ring.
Round 1: 3 ch (counts as 1 tr), 11 tr in ring, sl st to join, turn.
Round 2: 3 ch, 1 tr in same tr, 2 tr in each tr around, sl st to join, turn.
Round 3: 3 ch, 1 tr in same tr, 1 tr, (2 tr in next tr, 1 tr) around, sl st to join, turn.
Fasten off. Join yarn B in any st.
Round 4: 3 ch, 1 dtr in same st, 2 ch, (1 dtr, 1 tr) in next st, 1 tr, 1 htr, 3 dc, 1 htr, 1 tr, *(1 tr, 1 dtr) in same st, 2 ch, (1 dtr, 1 tr) in next st, 1 tr, 1 htr, 3 dc, 1 htr, 1 tr; rep from * twice more, sl st to join, turn.
Round 5: 3 ch (counts as first tr), work 1 tr in each st and (2 tr, 2 ch, 2 tr) in each corner 2ch-sp, around, sl st to join.
Round 6: *1 dc in each st to corner, (1 dc, 2 ch, 1 dc) in corner; rep from * 3 times, 1 dc in remaining sts, sl st to join. Fasten off.
Embroider face using yarn C.

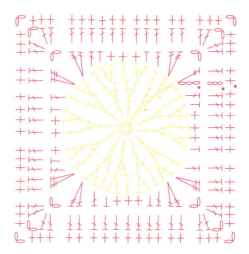

100 Essential Crochet Motifs

Motif 11:
Circle Granny Square

This lovely motif turns a circle into a square with a round of different-sized stitches.

Yarn A
208 Yellow Gold

Yarn B
522 Primrose

Yarn C
519 Freesia

Yarn D
256 Cornelia Rose

Yarn E
113 Delphinium

Yarn F
520 Lavender

Do not turn work throughout.
Using yarn A, 4 ch, sl st to 1st ch to form a ring.
Round 1: 3 ch (counts as 1 tr), 11 tr in ring, sl st to top of beg 3 ch to join. Fasten off.
Join yarn B to any st.
Round 2: 3 ch, 1 tr in same tr, 2 tr in each tr around, sl st to join. Fasten off.
Join yarn C to any st.
Round 3: 3 ch, 1 tr in same tr, 1 tr, (2 tr in next tr, 1 tr) around, sl st to join. Fasten off.
Join yarn D to any st.
Round 4: 3 ch, 1 tr in same tr, 2 tr, (2 tr in next tr, 2 tr) around, sl st to join. Fasten off.
Join yarn E to any st.
Round 5: 3 ch, 1 tr in same tr, 3 tr, (2 tr in next tr, 3 tr) around, sl st to join. Fasten off.
Join yarn F to any st.
Round 6: 4 ch (counts as 1 dtr), (1 dtr, 2 ch, 2 dtr) in same st, 1 dtr, 2 tr, 1 htr, 6 dc, 1 htr, 2 tr, 1 dtr, *(2 dtr, 2 ch, 2 dtr) in next st, 1 dtr, 2 tr, 1 htr, 6 dc, 1 htr, 2 tr, 1 dtr; rep from * twice more, sl st to join.
Round 7: *1 dc in each st to corner 2ch-sp, (1 dc, 2 ch, 1 dc) in corner 2ch-sp; rep from * 3 times, 1 dc in st to end of round, sl st to join. Fasten off.

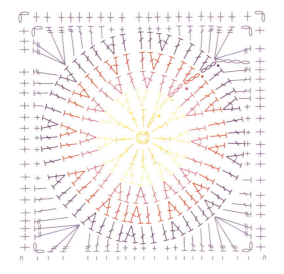

Motif 12:
Puff Stripe Square

This zesty square is the perfect introduction to using lots of pretty puff and beginning puff stitches.

Yarn A
392 Lime Juice

Yarn B
389 Apple Green

Do not turn work throughout.
Using yarn A: 6 ch, sl st to 1st ch to form a ring.
Round 1: 1 BegPuff, ch 3, 1 puff, ch 1, (1 puff, 3 ch, 1 BegPuff, 1 ch) 3 times, sl st to top of 3 ch to join. Fasten off.
Round 2: Join yarn B in corner 3ch-sp, (1 BegPuff, 3 ch, 1 puff) in same 3ch-sp, 2 ch, 3 tr in ch-sp, ch 2, *(1 puff, 3 ch, 1 puff) in corner 3ch-sp, 2 ch, 3 tr in ch-sp, ch 2; repeat from * twice more, sl st to first Beg Puff to join.
Round 3: Join yarn A in corner 3ch-sp, (1 BegPuff, 3 ch, 1 puff) in corner 3ch-sp, 2 ch, 2 tr in 2ch-sp, 1 tr in each tr to next 2ch-sp, 2 tr in 2ch-sp, *(1 puff, 3 ch, 1 puff) in corner 3ch-sp, 2 ch, 2 tr in 2ch-sp, 1 tr in each tr to next 2ch-sp, 2 tr in 2ch-sp, ch 2; repeat from * twice more, sl st to first puff to join.
Round 4: Rep round 3, using yarn B.
Round 5: Sl st into corner space, *(1 dc, 1 ch, 1 dc) in corner, 1 dc in each puff, ch-sp and tr to corner space; repeat from * 3 times, sl st to join. Fasten off.

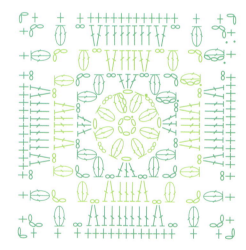

Notes
This motif uses beginning puff (BegPuff) and puff stitches. For instructions, see page 17.

100 Essential Crochet Motifs

Motif 13:
Purple Haze

This delicate square uses open corners and gorgeous purple shades to create its fabulous look.

Yarn A
226 Light Orchid

Yarn C
398 Colonial Rose

Yarn B
113 Delphinium

Do not turn work throughout.
Using yarn A, 10 ch, sl st to first st to form a ring.

Round 1: 3 ch (counts as 1 tr), 7 tr into ring, 2 ch, (8 tr, 2 ch) 3 times, sl st on top of 3 ch to join.

Round 2: Join yarn B in the first tr of any of the sets of 8 tr, *1 tr in each tr to corner, 6 ch, miss the 2 ch corner; rep from * 3 times, sl st to join.

Round 3: Join yarn C in the first tr of any of the sets of 8 tr, *1 tr in each tr to corner, 10 ch, miss the 6 ch corner; rep from * 3 times, sl st to join.

Round 4: Join yarn A in the first tr of any of the sets of 8 tr, *1 tr in each tr to corner, 14 ch, miss the 10 ch corner; rep from * 3 times, sl st to join. Fasten off.

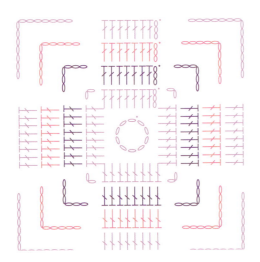

Motif 14:
Stained-glass Window Square

This square reminds me of the traditional stained glass windows in British churches.

Yarn A
519 Freesia

Yarn D
397 Cyan

Yarn B
110 Black

Yarn E
130 Old Lace

Yarn C
189 Royal Orange

Yarn F
256 Cornelia Rose

Using yarn A, 4 ch, sl st to join.
Round 1: 5 ch (counts as 1 tr, 2 ch), (1 tr, 2 ch) into ring 11 times, sl st to join.
Round 2: *(1 dc, 2 ch) in 2ch-sp between any tr; rep from * around, sl st to join.
Round 3: Using yarn C, 3 ch, 1 tr in any 2ch-sp, 1 ch, *(2 tr, 1 ch); rep from * in each 2ch-sp.
Round 4: Join yarn B in any dc from round 2, 4 ch (counts as 1 Sp-dc and 3 ch), *(1 Sp-dc in next dc from round 2, 3 ch); rep from *10 times, sl st to join.
Round 5: Join yarn D in any 3ch-sp from round 4, *(1 dc, 1 tr, 1 ch, 1 tr, 1 dc) in 3ch-sp; rep from *in each 3ch-sp, sl st into first dc to join, fasten off.
Round 6: Join yarn B in any ch-sp from round 5, 1 dc in ch-sp,*(2 ch, 1 Sp-dc in next Sp-dc from round 4, 2 ch, 1 dc in next ch-sp); rep from * 11 times, fasten off.
Round 7: Join yarn E in any Sp-dc from round 6, (4 ch, 1 tr, 1 ch, 1 tr) in top of first Sp-dc, then work (1 tr, 1 ch, 1 tr, 1 ch, 1 tr) in top of each Sp-dc around, sl st to join.
Round 8: Join yarn F in any ch-sp, (3 ch, 1 tr) in same ch-sp, 2 htr in next ch-sp, 2 dc in next 2ch-sp, 2 htr in next ch-sp, 2 tr in next ch-sp, miss 1 tr, (2 tr, 2 ch, 2 tr) in next ch-sp, miss 1 tr, *2 tr in next ch-sp, 2 htr in next ch-sp, 2 dc in next 2ch-sp, 2 htr in next ch-sp, 2 tr in next ch-sp, miss 1 tr, (2 tr, 2 ch, 2 tr) in next ch-sp, miss 1 tr; rep from * twice more, sl st to join, turn.
Round 9: *1 dc in each dc to corner, (1 dc, 2 ch, 1 dc) in corner; rep from * 3 times, 1 dc in remaining dc, sl st to join. Fasten off.

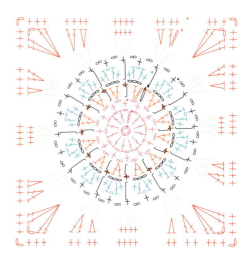

Notes
This motif uses spike double crochet stitches (Sp-dc). See page 19 for instructions.

100 Essential Crochet Motifs

Motif 15:
Spiky Circle

This motif uses the contrast between the open blue spokes and the round of pink half trebles and trebles.

Yarn A ■
520 Lavender

Yarn B ■
384 Powder Blue

Yarn C ■
604 Neon Pink

Yarn D ■
110 Black

Yarn E ■
130 Old Lace

Using yarn A, 4 ch, sl st to form a ring.
Round 1: 3 ch (counts as 1 tr), 15 tr in ring, sl st to top of 3 ch, turn (16 tr).
Fasten off. Join yarn B in any st.
Round 2: 5 ch (counts as 1 tr, 2 ch), (1 tr, 2 ch) in each tr around, sl st into top of beg 3 ch, turn.
Round 3: Join yarn C in any 2ch-sp, (3 ch, 2 tr, 2 ch, 3 tr, 1 ch) in same 2ch-sp, (3 htr, 1 ch) in next 3 2ch-sps, *(3 tr, 2 ch, 3 tr, 1 ch) in next 2ch-sp, (3 htr, 1 ch) in next 3 2ch-sp; rep from * twice more, sl st to top of beg 3 ch, turn.
Round 4: Join yarn D in any corner 2ch-sp, *(1 dc, 2 ch, 1 dc, 3 ch) in same corner 2ch-sp, (1 dc, 3 ch) in each ch-sp; rep from * 3 times, sl st into first dc.
Round 5: Join yarn E in any corner 2ch-sp, 3 ch (2 tr, 2 ch, 3 tr, 1 ch) in corner 2ch-sp, (3 tr, 1 ch) in each 3ch-sp to corner, *(3 tr, 2 ch, 3 tr, 1 ch) in corner ch-sp, (3 tr, 1 ch) in each 3ch-sp to corner; rep from * twice more, sl st to join. Fasten off.

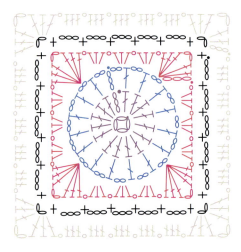

Motif 16:
Starburst Motif

This pretty circular motif can be made plain or in lots of different colourways.

Yarn A
604 Neon Pink

Yarn B
392 Lime Juice

Yarn C
519 Freesia

Yarn D
173 Bluebell

Yarn E
201 Electric Blue

Using yarn A, 4 ch, sl st to form a ring.
Round 1: 3 ch (counts as 1 tr), 15 tr in ring, sl st to top of 3ch, turn (16 tr).
Fasten off. Join yarn B in any st.
Round 2: Using yarn B, 1 BegPuff, 2 ch, (1 puff, 2 ch) around, sl st to join, turn.
Fasten off. Join yarn C in any ch-sp.
Round 3: (2 ch, tr3tog) in same ch-sp, 2 ch, (tr4tog, 2 ch, in next ch-sp) around, sl st to join, turn.
Fasten off. Join yarn D in any 2ch-sp.
Round 4: (2 ch, tr4tog) in same sp, 3 ch, (tr5tog, 3 ch, in next 2ch-sp) around, sl st to join, turn.
Fasten off. Join yarn E in any 3ch-sp.
Round 5: 4 ch (counts as 1 dtr), (2 dtr, 3 ch, 3 dtr) in same 3ch-sp, 3 tr in next 3ch-sp, 3 htr in next 3ch-sp, 3 tr in next 3ch-sp, *(3 dtr, 3 ch, 3 dtr) in next 3ch-sp, 3 tr in next 3ch-sp, 3 htr in next 3ch-sp, 3 tr in next 3ch-sp; rep from * twice more, sl st to join. Fasten off.

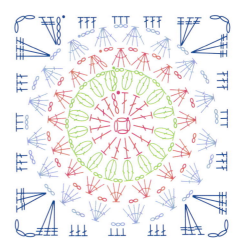

Notes
This motif uses beginning puff (BegPuff) and puff stitches. For instructions, see page 17.

Motif 17:
Starflower Square

This amazing square uses little puff stitches to create an interesting texture and a subtle star shape.

Yarn A
385 Crystalline

Do not turn work throughout.
Using yarn A, 4 ch, sl st to first st to form a ring.

Round 1: 3 ch, 11 tr in ring, join with sl st to top of beg 3 ch.

Round 2: Sl st into space between tr, 2 ch, 1 puff in same space, (1 ch, miss next tr, work puff st in sp before next tr) twice, 5 ch, miss next tr, *1 puff st in sp before next tr, (1 ch, miss next tr, work 1 puff st in space before next tr) twice, 5 ch, miss next tr; rep from * twice more, join with sl st in top of first puff.

Round 3: Sl st into ch-sp, 1 BegPuff in the same space, 1 ch, 1 puff st in the next ch-sp, 2 ch, 5 tr in the 5ch-sp, 2 ch *work 1 puff st in the next ch-sp, 1 ch, 1 puff st in the next ch-sp, 2 ch, 5 tr in next 5ch-sp, 2 ch; rep from * twice more, join with a sl st in top of the first puff.

Round 4: Sl st in first ch-sp, work 1 BegPuff in same sp, 2 ch, (1 tr in next tr, 1 ch) twice, (1 tr, 1 ch) 3 times in next tr, tr in next tr, 1 ch, 1 tr in next tr, *2 ch miss next 2ch-sp, 1 puff st in next ch-sp, 2 ch, miss next 2ch-sp, (1 tr in next tr, 1 ch) twice, (1 tr, 1 ch) 3 times in next tr, tr in next tr, 1 ch, 1 tr in next tr; rep from * twice more, 1 ch, miss last 2ch-sp, sl st in top of first puff st to form last 2ch-sp. Fasten off.

Notes

Motif 17
This motif uses beginning puff (BegPuff) and Puff stitches. For instructions, see page 17.

Motif 18
For instructions on raised triple treble front post stitches (rtrtrf), see page 18.

Motif 18:
Raised Treble Square

This motif is worked in the round, using raised triple treble front post stitches to create a gorgeous texture.

Yarn A
189 Royal Orange

Yarn C
397 Cyan

Yarn B
264 Light Coral

Yarn D
130 Old Lace

Do not turn work throughout.
Using yarn A, 4 ch, sl st to first st to form a ring.
Round 1: 3 ch, 2 tr, 2 ch, (3 tr, 2 ch) 3 times in ring, sl st to top of beg 3 ch to join, sl st to corner 2ch-sp.
Round 2: (3 ch, 2 tr, 2 ch, 3 tr) in 2ch-sp, 1 ch, *(3 tr, 2 ch, 3 tr) in next 2ch-sp, 1 ch; rep from * twice more, sl st to top of 3 ch, sl st to corner 2ch-sp.
Round 3: (3 ch, 2 tr, 2 ch, 3 tr) in 2ch-sp, 1 ch, (1 tr, 1 rtrtrf around 2nd of 3 tr in rnd 1, 1 tr) in next ch-sp, 1 ch, *(3 tr, 2 ch, 3 tr) in 2ch-sp, 1 ch, (1 tr, 1 rtrtrf around 2nd of 3 tr in rnd 1, 1 tr) in next ch-sp, 1 ch; rep from * twice more, sl st to top of beg 3 ch. Fasten off.
Round 4: Join yarn B (3 ch, 2 tr, 2 ch, 3 tr) in 2ch-sp, 1 ch, [(1 tr, 1 rtrtrf around 2nd of 3 tr in rnd 2, 1 tr) in next ch-sp, 1 ch] 2 times, *(3 tr, 2 ch, 3 tr) in 2ch-sp, 1 ch, [(1 tr, 1 rtrtrf in 2nd of 3 tr in rnd 2, 1 tr) in next ch-sp, 1 ch] 2 times; rep from * twice more, sl st in top of beg 3 ch, sl st to 2ch-sp.
Round 5: (3 ch, 2 tr, 2 ch, 3 tr) in 2ch-sp, 1 ch, (1 tr, 1 rtrtrf around 2nd of 3 tr in rnd 3, 1 tr) in next ch-sp, 1 ch, (1 tr, 1 rtrtrf around rtrtrf of rnd 3, 1 tr) in next ch-sp, 1 ch, (1 tr, 1 rtrtrf around 2nd of 3 tr in rnd 3, 1 tr) in next ch-sp, 1 ch, *(3 tr, 2 ch, 3 tr) in next 2ch-sp, 1 ch, (1 tr, 1 rtrtrf around 2nd of 3 tr in rnd 3, 1 tr) in next ch-sp, 1 ch, (1 tr, 1 rtrtrf around rtrtrf of rnd 3, 1 tr) in next ch-sp, 1 ch, (1 tr, 1 rtrtrf around 2nd of 3 tr in rnd 3, 1 tr) in next ch-sp, 1 ch; rep from * twice more, sl st to 3 ch. Fasten off.
Round 6: Join yarn C (3 ch, 2 tr, 2 ch, 3 tr) in 2ch-sp, 1 ch, *(1 tr, 1 rtrtrf around 2nd of 3 tr in rnd 4, 1 tr) in next ch-sp, 1 ch, [(1 tr, 1 rtrtrf around rtrtrf of rnd 4, 1 tr) in next ch-sp, 1 ch] 2 times, (1 tr, 1 rtrtrf around 2nd of 3 tr in rnd 4, 1 tr) in next ch-sp, 1 ch, **(3 tr, 2 ch, 3 tr) in 2ch-sp; rep from * twice more ending last rep at **, sl st in top of beg 3 ch, sl st to 2ch-sp.

Round 7: (3 ch, 2 tr, 2 ch, 3 tr) in 2ch-sp, 1 ch, *(1 tr, 1 rtrtrf around 2nd of 3 tr in rnd 5, 1 tr) in ch-sp, 1 ch, [(1 tr, 1 rtrtrf around rtrtrf of rnd 5, 1 tr) in ch-sp, 1 ch] 3 times, (1 tr, 1 rtrtrf around 2nd of 3 tr in rnd 5, 1 tr) in next ch-sp, 1 ch, **(3 tr, 2 ch, 3 tr) in 2ch-sp; rep from * twice more ending last rep at **, sl st to top of 3 ch. Fasten off.
Round 8: Using yarn D, rep rnd 7 working into each ch-sp around and working rtrtrf sts into rnd 6, sl st to 3 ch.
Round 9: *1 dc in each tr to corner space (miss the ch-sp), (1 dc, 2 ch, 1 dc) in 2ch-sp; rep from * 3 times, 1 dc in each of remaining dc sts, sl st to join. Fasten off.

100 Essential Crochet Motifs

Motif 19:
Small Sunflower Square

This lovely motif uses a round of treble 3 togethers to create a sunflower petal effect.

Yarn A ■
503 Hazelnut

Yarn C ■
515 Emerald

Yarn B ■
522 Primrose

Turn after each round.
Using yarn A, 4 ch, sl st to form a ring.
Round 1: 3 ch (counts as 1 tr), 15 tr in ring, sl st to join. Fasten off.
Join yarn B in any stitch.
Round 2: 2 ch, tr2tog in next 2 sts (counts as tr3tog), *3 ch, place the hook in the same space as last tr, and using the next 2 stitches tr3tog in these 3 stitches; rep from * 6 times, 3 ch, sl st in the top of the first tr3tog. Fasten off.
Round 3: Join yarn C in any 3ch-sp, 3 ch (counts as 1 tr), (2 tr, 2 ch, 3 tr) in 3ch-sp, 5 tr in next 3ch-sp, *(3 tr, 2 ch, 3 tr) in next 3ch-sp, 5 tr in next 3ch-sp; rep from * twice more, sl st to join. Fasten off.

Motif 20:
Sherbet Surprise

Use sherbet shades in this fabulous double crochet square that's easy to scale up to a bigger project.

Yarn A
100 Lemon Chiffon

Yarn B
264 Light Coral

Yarn C
222 Tulip

Yarn D
114 Shocking Pink

Yarn E
520 Lavender

Yarn F
511 Cornflower

Do not turn work throughout.
Using yarn A, 4 ch, sl st to first st to form a ring.
Round 1: 8 dc into ring, sl st to join.
Round 2: *(1 dc, 2 ch, 1 dc) in next st, dc in next st; rep from * 3 times, sl st to join, fasten off.
Round 3: Join yarn B in any 2ch-sp, *(1 dc, 2 ch, 1 dc) in corner space, 1 ch, miss 1 dc, 1 dc in next st, ch 1; rep from * 3 times.
Round 4: Join yarn C, in any 2ch-sp, **(1 dc, 2 ch, 1 dc) in corner space, *1 ch, miss 1 dc, 1 dc; rep from * to corner space, rep from** 3 times, sl st to join.
Rounds 5–13: Rep round 4, changing colours each round: D, E, F, A, B, C, D, E, F.
Fasten off.

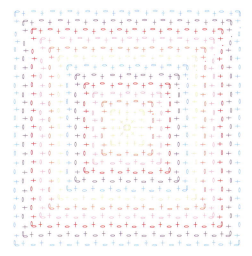

100 Essential Crochet Motifs

Motif 21:
African Violet Square

This motif uses spike treble stitches to outline the petals of this lovely design.

Yarn A ■
256 Cornelia Rose

Yarn B ■
520 Lavender

Yarn C ■
113 Delphinium

Yarn D ■
130 Old Lace

Using yarn A, 4 ch, sl st to form a ring.
Round 1: 3 ch (counts as 1 tr), 1 tr in ring, 1 ch, (2 tr, 1 ch) seven times in ring, sl st to top of beg 3 ch to join, turn.
Round 2: Join in yarn B in any ch-sp: 3 ch, (1 tr, 2 ch, 2 tr) in same ch-sp, (2 tr, 2 ch, 2 tr) in each ch-sp around, sl st to top of beg 3 ch to join, turn. Do not fasten off.
Round 3: Sl st to next 2ch-sp, 3 ch, 6 tr in same 2ch-sp, 7 tr in each rem 2ch-sp around, sl st to top of beg 3 ch to join, turn.
Round 4: Join yarn C to first of any 7tr, *1 dc in each of next 7 tr, 1 Sp-tr in space between 2 tr groups below in row 2; rep from * around, sl st to first dc to join, do not turn.
Round 5: Join yarn D in any Sp-tr of rnd 4, 6 ch (counts as 1 dtr, 2 ch), 1 dtr in same st, 2 tr, 1 htr, 4 dc, 1 htr in Sp-tr, 4 dc, 1 htr, 2 tr, *(1 dtr, 2 ch, 1 dtr) in next Sp-tr, 2 tr, 1 htr, 4 dc, 1 htr in Sp-tr, 4 dc, 1 htr, 2 tr; rep from * twice more, sl st to join.
Round 6: *1 dc in each dc to corner, (1 dc, 2 ch, 1 dc) in corner; rep from * 3 times, 1 dc in remaining sts, sl st to join.

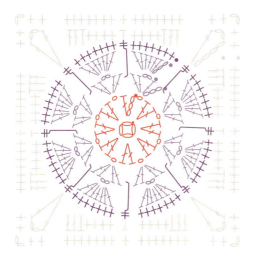

Notes
Spike treble (Sp-tr) stitches are worked by hooking yarn 2 rounds below the current round. For instructions, see page 19.

Motif 22:
Mitred Flower

This little square combines a cute little granny square and simple treble stitches to create a mitred look.

Yarn A
189 Royal Orange

Yarn B
256 Cornelia Rose

Yarn C
384 Powder Blue

Yarn D
249 Saffron

Yarn E
130 Old Lace

Using yarn A, 4 ch, sl st to first ch to form a ring.
Round 1: 4 ch (counts as 1 tr, 1 ch), (1 tr, 1 ch) 7 times in ring, sl st to 3rd of 4 ch to join, turn.
Fasten off. Join yarn B in any ch-sp.
Round 2: 3 ch, 2 tr in same ch-sp, 1 ch, (3 tr, 1 ch) in each of next 7 ch-sps around, sl st to top of 3 ch to join, turn.
Fasten off.
Join yarn C in any ch-sp.
Round 3: 3 ch, (2 tr, 2 ch, 3 tr) in same ch-sp, 3 tr in next ch-sp, *(3 tr, 2 ch, 3 tr) in next ch-sp, 3 tr in next ch-sp; rep from * twice more, sl st to top of beg 3 ch to join.
Fasten off.

The rest of the square is made by working on just two sides of the square and turning each round.
Join yarn D in any corner space.
Round 1: 3 ch, 1 tr in same corner 2ch-sp, 3 tr in each sp between 3 tr groups to corner, (3 tr, 2 ch, 3 tr) in corner space, 3 tr in each space between 3 tr groups to corner, 2 tr in corner 2ch-sp. Fasten off, turn.
Round 2: Using Yarn E, 3 ch in top of last tr from last round, miss 1 tr, 3 tr in each space between 3 tr to corner, (3 tr, 2 ch, 3 tr) in corner space, 3 tr in each space between tr to corner, 1 tr in corner space.
Round 3: Repeat round 1 using yarn A.
Round 4: Using yarn B, 3 ch, 1 tr in each tr to corner space, (2 tr, 2 ch, 2 tr) in corner space, 1 tr in each tr made in previous round.
Round 5: Using yarn C, rep round 4.

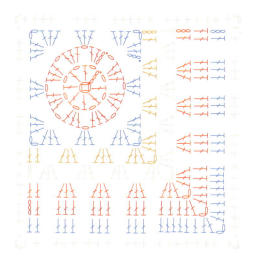

Round 6: Working around entire square this round, join Yarn E in corner space, work (1 dc, 2 ch, 1 dc) in corner space and then work 1 dc in each tr to last tr, in the last tr work (1 dc, 2 ch, 1 dc), *evenly distribute 17 sts down the next side of square, (1 dc, 2 ch, 1 dc) in corner space; rep from * once more, 1 dc in each tr to next corner space, sl st to join. Fasten off.

Motif 23:
Snowflake Square

Warm up the winter months with this lovely snowflake square in festive red.

Yarn A
130 Old Lace

Yarn B
115 Hot Red

Using yarn A, 4 ch, sl st to join.

Round 1: 3 ch, 15 tr into ring, sl st to join, turn.

Round 2: 5 ch (5 ch counts as 1 tr, 2 ch), 1 tr in same tr, miss 1 tr, *(1 tr, 2 ch, 1 tr), miss 1 tr; rep from * 7 times, sl st to join, turn.

Round 3: Sl st into 2ch-sp, 3 ch (1 tr, 2 ch, 2 tr) in 2ch-sp, (2 tr, 2 ch, 2 tr) in each 2ch-sp around, sl st into top of the 3rd ch made in first 5 ch, turn.

Round 4: Sl st into 2ch-sp, 3 ch (counts as 1 tr), (2 tr, 2 ch, 3 tr) in same 2ch-sp, (3 tr, 2 ch, 3 tr) in each 2ch-sp around, sl st into top of 3 ch to join, turn.

Round 5: Sl st into 2ch-sp, 3 ch (counts as 1 tr), (3 tr, 2 ch, 4 tr, 1 ch) in same 2ch-sp, (4 tr, 2 ch, 4 tr, 1 ch), in each 2ch-sp around, sl st into top of 3rd ch to join, turn.

Round 6: Join yarn B in any corner 2ch-sp, 3 ch (1 tr, 2 ch, 2 tr) in 2ch-sp, 1 tr in each of the next 6 tr, 1 htr in next tr, 1 dc in next tr, 1 sl st in 2ch-sp, 1 dc in next tr, 1 htr in next tr, 1 tr in next 6 tr to corner, *(2 tr, 2 ch, 2 tr) in corner 2ch-sp, 1 tr in each of the next 6 tr, 1 htr in next tr, 1 dc in next tr, 1 sl st in 2ch-sp, 1 dc in next tr, 1 htr in next tr, 1 tr in next 6 tr to corner; rep from * twice more, sl st to join. Don't turn.

Round 7: Sl st to 2ch-sp, *(2 tr, 2 ch, 2 tr) in same 2ch-sp, 1 tr in each tr to corner space; rep from * 3 times, sl st to join. Fasten off.

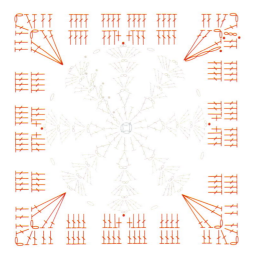

Motif 24:
Half Rainbow

This little half rainbow motif combines traditional colour schemes with a pretty pink edging.

Yarn A
130 Old lace

Yarn B
384 Powder Blue

Yarn C
389 Apple Green

Yarn D
280 Lemon

Yarn E
410 Rich Coral

Yarn F
256 Cornelia Rose

Yarn G
222 Tulip

Using yarn A, 4 ch (counts as 1 tr, 1 ch).
Row 1: 2 tr in 4th ch from hook, turn.
Row 2: 3 ch, (counts as 1 tr) 1 tr in same tr, 2 tr in each of next 2 sts, turn.
Row 3: Using yarn B, 3 ch, 2 tr in next st, *1 tr in next st, 2 tr in next st; rep from *, turn.
Row 4: Using yarn C, 3 ch, 1 tr in next st, 2 tr in next st, *1 tr in next 2 st, 2 tr in next st; rep from *, turn.
Row 5: Using yarn D, 3 ch, 1 tr in next 2 sts, 2 tr in next st, *1 tr in next 3 sts, 2 tr in next st; rep from *, turn.
Row 6: Using yarn E, 3 ch, 1 tr in next 3 sts, 2 tr in next st, *1 tr in next 4 sts, 2 tr in next st; rep from *, turn.
Row 7: Using yarn F, 3 ch, 1 tr in next 4 sts, 2 tr in next st, *1 tr in next 5 sts, 2 tr in next st; rep from *, turn.
Row 8: Using Yarn A, 3 ch, 1 tr in next 5 sts, 2 tr in next st, *1 tr in next 6 sts, 2 tr in next st; rep from *, turn.
Row 9: 1 ch (does not count as st), 1 dc in first tr, 1 dc in next 3 sts, 1 htr in next 4 sts , 1 tr in next 4 sts, 1 dtr in next st, 2 ch, 1 dtr in next st, 1 tr in next 4 sts, 1 htr in next 4 sts, 1 dc in next 4 sts, turn.
Row 10: 1 ch (does not count as st), 1 dc in first st, 1 dc in next 3 sts, 1 htr in next 4 sts , 1 tr in next 4 sts, (1 dtr, 2 ch, 1 dtr) in 2ch-sp, 1 tr in next 4 sts, 1 htr in next 4 sts, 1 dc in the next 4 sts, turn.
Round 11: Using yarn G, 3 ch, (2 tr, 2 ch, 3 tr) in 2ch-sp, 1 ch, miss 3 sts, (3 tr in next st, 1 ch, miss 2 sts) 3 times, (3 tr, 3 ch, 3 tr) in the last dc on corner of row, 1 ch, miss next 2 rows, 3 tr in st on row end of row 7, 1 ch, miss 1 row end, 3 tr around st on row 5, 1 ch, miss 1 row end, 3 tr on st at end of row 3, 1 ch, (3 tr, 2 ch, 3 tr) into 1 ch of original 4 ch made in row 1, 1 ch, miss 2 row ends, 3 tr in top of st at end of row 3, 1 ch, 3 tr on st at end of row 5, 1 ch, 3 tr in top of row 7, 1 ch, (3 tr, 2 ch, 3 tr) all into top of corner of last st of row 9 (on the corner), (1 ch, miss 2 sts, 3 tr into next st) 3 times, 1 ch, sl st into top of 3 ch, turn.
Round 12: *1 dc in each tr and ch-sp to corner space, (1 dc, 2 ch, 1 dc) in corner space; rep from * 3 times, 1 dc in each of the remaining sts and ch-spaces, sl st to join.

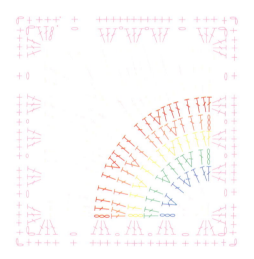

100 Essential Crochet Motifs

Motif 25:
Sun Square

This sunny square uses treble 3 togethers to create the points of the sun at its centre.

Yarn A
208 Yellow Gold

Yarn C
604 Neon Pink

Yarn B
384 Powder Blue

Using yarn A, 4 ch, sl st to form a ring.
Round 1: 3 ch (counts as 1 tr), 11 tr in ring, sl st to join, turn.
Round 2: (3 ch, 1 tr) in same tr, 2 tr in each tr around, sl st to join, turn.
Round 3: 2 ch (counts as the first part of a tr3tog), tr2tog, miss 1 tr, 3 ch, *(tr3tog, 3 ch), miss 1 tr, 3 ch; rep around, sl st to join, do not turn.
Round 4: Using yarn A, 3 ch in yarn A (counts as 1 tr) in the top of any tr3tog.
Change to yarn B: 3 tr in 3ch-sp.
*Change to yarn A: 1 tr in top of tr3tog.
Change to yarn B: 3 tr in 3ch-sp; rep from *around, sl st to join.
Fasten off yarn A, do not turn.
Round 5: 1 ch, *1 dc, 1 htr in each of next 2 sts, 1 tr in each of next 2 sts, 1 dtr in next st, (2 dtr, 2 ch, 2 dtr) in next st, 1 dtr in next st, 1 tr in next 2 sts, 1 htr in next 2 sts; rep from * 3 times, sl st to join. Fasten off, do not turn.
Round 6: Join yarn C in any corner 2ch-sp, 3 ch, (2 tr, 2 ch, 3 tr) in corner space, 1 tr in each tr to corner 2ch-sp, *(3 tr, 2 ch, 3 tr) in 2ch-sp, 1 tr in each tr to corner space; rep from * twice more, sl st to join. Fasten off.

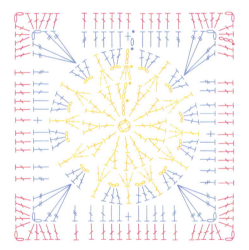

100 Essential Crochet Motifs

Motif 26:
Moon Child

You could pair the Sun Square with this wonderful half moon to keep with the celestial theme.

Yarn A
261 Capri Blue

Yarn C
384 Powder Blue

Yarn B
280 Lemon

Do not turn work throughout.
Using yarn A, 4 ch, sl st to first st to form a ring.
Round 1: 3 ch (counts as 1 tr), 11 tr into ring, sl st to join.
Round 2: 3 ch, 1 tr in same tr, 2 tr in each tr around sl st to first tr.
Round 3: 1 ch (doesn't count as a st), 2 dc in first tr, 1 dc in next tr, 2 dc in next st.
Join in yarn B on next st and carry yarn A underneath sts for this round. In yarn B, 1 dc in next st, 2 dc in next st, 1 htr, 2 htr, 1 tr, 2 tr, 1 dtr, 2 dtr, 1 dtr, 1 triple tr, 1 dtr, 2 dtr, 1 dtr, 2 tr, 1 tr, 2 htr, 1 htr, 2 dc, 1 dc.
Join in yarn A and cut yarn B. In yarn A, 2 dc, 1 dc, sl st into first dc in round.
Round 4: 3 ch (counts as 1 tr) 1 tr in next 4 sts, (1 tr, 1 dtr, 2 ch, 1 dtr, 1 tr) in next st to make a corner, 1 tr, 2 htr, 4 dc, 1 htr, (1 tr, 1 dtr, 2 ch, 1 dtr, 1 tr) in next st, 1 htr, 1 dc, 4 sl st, 1 htr, (1 tr, 1 dtr, 2 ch, 1 dtr, 1 tr) in next st, 1 htr, 4 dc, 1 htr, 2 dc, (1 tr, 1 dtr, 2 ch, 1 dtr, 1 tr) in next st, 1 dc in next 4 sts, sl st to join.
Round 5: 3 ch, *1 tr in each st to corner 2ch-sp, (2 tr, 2 ch, 2 tr) in corner space; rep from * 3 times, 1 tr in remaining tr, sl st to join, fasten off.
Round 6: Join yarn C in any corner 2ch-sp, 3 ch (1 tr, 2 ch, 2 tr) in corner space, 1 tr in each tr to next corner sp, *(2 tr, 2 ch, 2 tr) in corner sp, 1 tr in each tr to next corner sp; rep from * twice more, sl st to join. Fasten off.

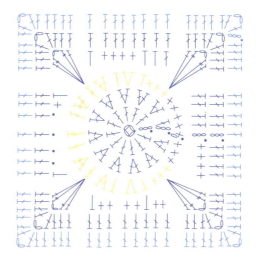

Notes
For instructions on triple treble (trtr), see page 15.

Motif 27:
Twinkle Twinkle Little Star

Staying in the sky for this tiny star-shaped square, you can opt for traditional colours or mix it up a bit.

Yarn A
280 Lemon

Yarn C
410 Rich Coral

Yarn B
173 Bluebell

Do not turn work throughout
Using yarn A, 4 ch, sl st to first st to form a ring.

Round 1: 3 ch (counts as 1 tr), 14 tr in ring, sl st to top of beg 3 ch to join.

Round 2: *5 ch, 1 dc in second ch from hook, 1 htr in next ch, 1 tr in next ch, 1 dtr in next, miss 2 tr, sl st into next st; rep from * 4 times, sl st to join, fasten off.

Round 3: Join yarn B in top of any star point with *1 dc, working into the blo on this side of point and into chain on the other work as folls: 1 htr, 1 tr, 1 etr, dtr2tog, 1 etr, 1 tr, 1 htr; rep from * 4 times, sl st into the top of the first dc to join.

Round 4: 1 ch (counts as 1 htr) at top of star, 1 dc in each of the next 3 sts, 1 htr, 1 tr, 1 etr, (1 dtr, 2 ch, 1 dtr) in next st, *1 etr, 1 tr, 1 htr, 1 dc in next 3 sts, 1 htr, 1 tr, 1 etr, (1 dtr, 2 ch, 1 dtr) in next st; rep from * twice more, 1 etr, 1 tr, sl st in top of first ch, fasten off.

Round 5: Join yarn C in any corner space, 3 ch, (1 tr, 2 ch, 2 tr) in same corner space, 1 tr in each tr to corner, *(2 tr, 2 ch, 2 tr) in same corner space, 1 tr in each tr to corner; rep from * twice more, sl st to join, fasten off.

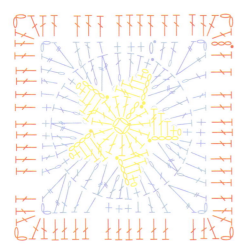

Notes
This motif uses extended treble stitch (etr).
For instructions, see page 14.
To get the raised star effect, stitches in round 3 are worked in the back loop only (blo), see page 15.

Motif 28:
Josie's Little Flower

Poppies were my late mother's favourite flower, so I've dedicated this little 3D flower to her.

Yarn A
507 Chocolate

Yarn C
238 Powder Pink

Yarn B
390 Poppy Rose

Do not turn work throughout.
Using yarn A, 4 ch, sl st to form a ring.
Round 1: 4 ch (counts as 1 tr, 1 ch), (1 tr, 1 ch) 7 times in ring, sl st to join. Fasten off.
Round 2: Join yarn B with sl st to any ch-sp, (1 dc, 2 tr, 1 dc) in each ch-sp around (8 petals).
Round 3: Working behind petals made on round 2, insert hook from back to front to back, work 1 sl st behind first tr of round 1, *3 ch, inserting hook from back to front to back work 1 dc around next tr; rep from * around (8 x 3ch-sps).
Round 4: Sl st in next 3ch-sp, (1 dc, 1 htr, 3 tr, 1 htr, 1 dc) in each 3ch-sp around.
Round 5: Working behind petals made on Round 4, inserting hook from back to front to back, sl st behind next dc made on round 3, *4 ch, 1 dc around next dc on round 3; rep from * around.
Round 6: Rep Round 4 working in each 4ch-sp.
Round 7: Working behind petals made on round 6, sl st behind next dc from round 5, *5 ch, 1 dc around dc from round 5; rep from * around, fasten off.
Round 8: Join yarn C in any 5ch-sp, 3 ch (counts as 1 tr), (2 tr, 2 ch, 3 tr) in same 5ch-sp, 3 tr in next 5ch-sp, *(3 tr, 2 ch, 3 tr) in next 5ch-sp, 3 tr in next 5ch-sp; rep from * twice more, sl st to join.
Round 9: 3 ch (counts as 1 tr), 1 tr in each tr to corner 2ch-sp, *(2 tr, 2 ch, 2 tr) in corner 2ch-sp, 1 tr in each tr to next corner 2ch-sp; rep from * twice more, (2 tr, 2 ch, 2 tr) in next corner 2ch-sp, 1 tr in each st to end, sl st to join. Fasten off.

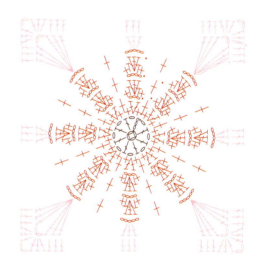

Motif 29:
Mixed Stitch Motif

This vibrant motif looks beautiful made into a blanket or an item of clothing.

Yarn A ■
520 Lavender

Yarn B ■
115 Hot Red

Yarn C ■
246 Icy Pink

Yarn D ■
247 Bluebird

Yarn E ■
509 Baby Blue

Yarn F ■
164 Light Navy

Yarn G ■
130 Old Lace

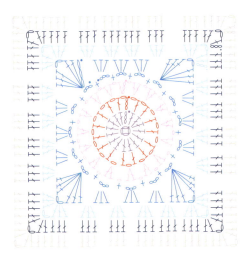

Turn at end of each round.
Using yarn A, 4 ch, sl st to first st to form a ring.
Round 1: 3 ch (counts as 1 tr) 15 tr in ring, sl st to top of beg 3 ch to join, turn (16 tr). Fasten off.
Join yarn B in any tr.
Round 2: 4 ch (counts as 1 tr, 1 ch), (1 tr, 1 ch) in each tr around, sl st to 3rd of beg 4 ch, turn. Fasten off.
Round 3: Join yarn C in any ch-sp, 3 ch, (1 tr, 1 ch) in same ch-sp, (2 tr, 1 ch) in each ch-sp around, sl st to top of beg 3 ch, turn. Fasten off.
Round 4: Join yarn D in any ch-sp, (1 dc, 3 ch) in each ch-sp around, sl st to join, turn, don't fasten off.
Round 5: Sl st in 3ch-sp, (3 ch, 2 tr, 2 ch, 3 tr) in same 3ch-sp, 3 htr in next 3 3ch-sps, *(3 tr, 2 ch, 3 tr) in next 3ch-sp, 3 htr in next 3 3ch-sps; rep from * twice more, sl st to top of beg 3 ch, turn. Fasten off.
Round 6: Join yarn E in any corner 2ch-sp, (3 ch, 2 tr, 2 ch, 3 tr) in corner 2ch-sp, 3 tr in space between each 3 htr group to next corner 2ch-sp, *(3 tr, 2 ch, 3 tr) in 2ch-sp, 3 tr in space between each 3 htr group to next corner 2ch-sp; rep from * twice more, sl st to top of beg 3 ch, turn. Fasten off.
Round 7: Join yarn F in any corner 2ch-sp, (3 ch, 1 tr, 2 ch, 2 tr) in corner 2ch-sp, 1 tr in each st to next corner 2ch-sp, *(2 tr, 2 ch, 2 tr) in corner 2ch-sp, 1 tr in each st to next corner 2ch-sp; rep from * twice more, sl st to join, turn. Fasten off.
Round 8: Using yarn G, repeat round 7. Fasten off.

Motif 30:
Block By Block

This eye-catching motif is made up of lots of little motifs, joined as you go or sewn together.

Yarn A
280 Lemon

Yarn B
386 Peach

Yarn C
222 Tulip

Yarn D
397 Cyan

Yarn E
520 Lavender

Yarn F
385 Crystalline

Yarn G
130 Old Lace

Do not turn work throughout.
Using yarn A, 4 ch, sl st to first st to form a ring.
Round 1: (3 ch (counts as 1 tr) 2 tr, 2 ch) into ring,*3 tr, 2 ch into ring; rep from * twice more, sl st to join. Fasten off.
Repeat for yarns B, C, D, E, F. See notes, below.
For subsequent squares, join by replacing 2 ch in corner of squares with (1 ch, sl st in 2ch-space on adjacent square, 1 ch).

Once all squares are joined (4x4 squares), make border.

Border
With the right side of work facing you, join yarn G in corner space.
Round 1: 3 ch (counts as 1 tr), (1 tr, 2 ch, 2 tr) in corner space, 1 tr in each corner and tr of mini motifs to corner space, *(2 tr, 2 ch, 2 tr) in corner space, 1 tr in each corner and tr of mini motifs to corner space; rep from * twice more, sl st to join. Fasten off.

Notes
Mini motifs are joined using the join-as-you-go method: make the first motif then join each square together with sl st as you work. If you prefer, you can sew the motifs together using a neat whip stitch (see page 21).

Make 3 motifs in yarns A, B, C and D
Make 2 motifs in yarns E and F
16 in total arranged 4 x 4

Motif 31:
Retro Flower Motif

Give your project some vintage vibes with these gorgeous retro flower motifs.

Yarn A ■
157 Root Beer

Yarn B ■
280 Lemon

Yarn C ■
264 Light Coral

Yarn D ■
114 Shocking Pink

Yarn E ■
238 Powder Pink

Using yarn A, 6 ch, sl st to first ch to form a ring.
Round 1: 8 dc into ring, sl st to join, turn.
Round 2: 1 ch (does not count as a st), 1 dc in next dc, 1 ch, (1 dc, 1 ch) in each dc around, sl st to join, turn. Fasten off. Join yarn B in any ch-sp.
Round 3: 3 ch (counts as first tr), 2 tr in same ch-sp, 1 ch, (3 tr, 1 ch) in each ch-sp around, sl st to join, turn. Fasten off. Join yarn C in top of first tr of any 3 tr group.
Round 4: 3 ch (counts as first tr of tr2tog), 1 tr in next tr, starting in same tr as last tr work tr2tog over next 2 tr, 2 ch, *tr2tog over next 2 tr, 3 ch, starting in same tr as last tr work tr2tog over next 2 tr, 2 ch; rep from * around, sl st to top of first 3 ch, turn. Fasten off.
Join yarn D in any 2ch-sp.
Round 5: *1 dc in 2ch-sp, (3 tr, 1 ch, 3 tr) in 3ch-sp; rep from * around, sl st to join, turn. Fasten off.
Join yarn E in any ch-sp.
Round 6: *1 dc in ch-sp, 1 ch, miss 3 tr, (2 tr, 2 ch, 2 tr) in 1 dc, 2 ch, miss 3 tr; rep from * 7 times, sl st in first dc, do not turn.
Round 7: 4 ch (counts as 1 dtr), (2 dtr, 2 ch, 3 dtr) in same dc to make corner, 1 ch, miss next 2 ch and next 2 tr, 2 dc in next 2ch-sp, 1 dc in each of next 2 tr, 1 dc in next 1 ch-sp, 1 dc in next dc, 1 dc in next 2ch-sp, 1 dc in each of next 2 tr, 2 dc in next 2ch-sp, 1 ch, miss next 2 tr and next 1 ch-sp, *(3 dtr, 2 ch, 3 dtr) in next dc to make corner, 1 ch, miss next 2 ch and next 2 tr, 2 dc in next 2ch-sp, 1 dc in each of next 2 tr, 1 dc in next 1 ch-sp, 1 dc in next dc, 1 dc in next 2ch-sp, 1 dc in each of next 2 tr, 2 dc in next 2ch-sp, 1 ch, miss next 2 tr and next 1 ch-sp; rep from * twice more, sl st to join. Fasten off.

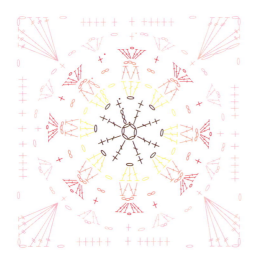

100 Essential Crochet Motifs

Motif 32:
Cluster Triangle Square

This square uses clusters of 6 stitches to create this dramatic triangle effect.

Yarn A
398 Colonial Rose

Yarn B
520 Lavender

Yarn C
513 Apple Granny

Yarn D
130 Old Lace

Using yarn A, 6 ch, sl st to first st to form a ring.
Round 1: 3 ch (counts as 1 tr), 5 tr, 3 ch into ring,*6 tr, 3 ch into ring; rep from * twice more, sl st to join, turn.
Round 2: Join yarn B in the top of the first tr of any of the 6 tr crochet, 3 ch, tr5tog, worked across next 5 sts, *4 ch, sl st in 3ch-sp, 4 ch, tr6tog worked across next 6 sts; rep from * twice more, 4 ch, sl st in 3ch-sp, 4 ch, join with a sl st into the top of beg 3 ch, turn.
Round 3: Join yarn C in the top of any tr6tog with a sl st, *working over sts in round 2, (6 tr, 3 ch, 6 tr) in next 3ch-sp of round 1, sl st in top of next tr6tog; rep from * 3 times, sl st in top of first sl st, fasten off, turn.
Round 4: Join yarn D in any corner 3ch-sp, 3 ch, (1 tr, 3 ch, 2 tr) in same corner 3ch-sp, 1 tr in each tr and the top of tr6tog to corner, *(2 tr, 3 ch, 2 tr) in same corner space, 1 tr in each tr and the top of tr6tog to corner; rep from * twice more, sl st to join. Fasten off.

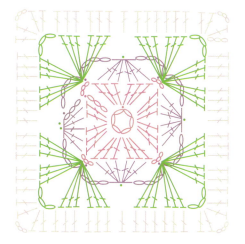

Motif 33:
Carnation Square

This square uses popcorn stitches to create its gorgeous, three-dimensional petals.

Yarn A
280 Lemon

Yarn C
130 Old Lace

Yarn B
246 Icy Pink

Do not turn work throughout.
Using yarn A, 6 ch, sl st to first st to form a ring.
Round 1: 1 ch (does not count as a st), 8 dc into ring, join with a sl st.
Round 2: Join yarn B in the top of any dc, (1 BegPop, 2ch) in first dc, (1 pop, 2 ch) in each st around, join with a sl st to first pop.
Round 3: Sl st into first ch-sp, (1 BegPop, 2 ch, 1 pop, 2 ch) in same ch-sp, *(1 pop, 2 ch, 1 pop, 2 ch) in next ch-sp; rep from *6 times, join with a sl st in the top of the first pop.
Round 4: Sl st in first 2ch-sp, (1 BegPop, 2 ch, 1 pop) in same 2ch-sp, 2 ch, (1 pop, 2 ch) in next 2ch-sp; rep from *7 times, join with a sl st to top of first pop, fasten off.
Round 5: Join yarn C in any 2ch-sp, 3 ch (counts as 1 tr), (1 tr, 1 dtr, 2 ch, 1 dtr, 2 tr) in the same 2ch-sp, 2 tr in next 2ch-sp, (1 tr, 1 htr) in next 2ch-sp, 2 tr in next 2ch-sp, *(2 tr, 1 dtr, 2 ch, 1 dtr, 2 tr) in next 2ch-sp, 2 tr in next 2ch-sp, (1 tr, 1 htr) in next 2ch-sp, 2 htr in next 2ch-sp, (1 htr, 1 tr) in next 2ch-sp; rep from * twice more, join with a sl st in the top of beg 3 ch.
Round 6: *1 dc in each st to corner space, (1 dc, 2 ch, 1 dc) in corner space; rep from * 3 times, 1 dc in remaining sts, sl st to join, fasten off.

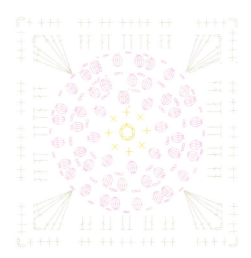

Notes
Popcorn (pop) stitches are used to create a raised effect. Beginning pop stitches (BegPop) use 3ch for the first tr in a pop. For instructions, see p 17.

Motif 34:
Mini 3D Flower

This little popcorn flower is so cute it adds texture to a project with its perfect little popcorns.

Yarn A
280 Lemon

Yarn C
130 Old Lace

Yarn B
520 Lavender

Do not turn work throughout.
Using yarn A, 4 ch, sl st to first st to form a ring.
Round 1: 1 ch (does not count as a st), 6 dc into ring, join with a sl st.
Round 2: join yarn B in the top of any dc, 1 BegPop, 2 ch, (1 pop, 2 ch) in each remaining st around, join with a sl st to first pop, fasten off.
Round 3: Join yarn C in the back loop of any of the pops, 3 ch (counts as 1 tr), *(2 tr, 1 dtr, 2 ch, 1 dtr, 2 tr) in next ch-sp, 1 tr in the back of next petal, 2 tr in next ch-sp, (2 tr, 1 dtr, 2 ch, 1 dtr, 2 tr) in back of next petal, 2 tr in next ch-sp, ** 1 tr in back of next petal; rep from * twice more ending last rep at **, join with a sl st in top of beg chain. Fasten off.

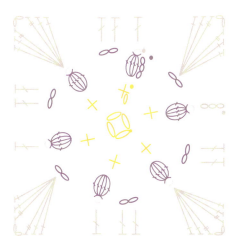

> **Notes**
> Popcorn (pop) stitches are used to create a raised effect. Beginning pop stitches (BegPop) use 3ch for the first tr in a pop. For instructions, see p 17.

Motif 35:
Kaleidoscope Square

This unusual square uses raised chain loops. It's like looking through the lens of a kaleidoscope.

Yarn A
114 Shocking Pink

Yarn B
253 Tropic

Yarn C
520 Lavender

Yarn D
245 Green Yellow

Yarn E
130 Old Lace

Do not turn work throughout.
Using yarn A, 4 ch, sl st to first st to form a ring.

Round 1: 5 ch (counts as corner 2ch-sp and 1 tr), 2 tr in ring, work ch loop, *1 tr in ring, 2 ch, 2 tr in ring, work ch loop; repeat from * twice more; join with a sl st to third ch of first 5 ch.

Round 2: Join yarn B in any 2ch-sp, 7 ch (counts as 1 tr, 4 ch), 2 tr in same 2ch-sp, tr in next 2 tr, ch-loop, tr in next tr, *(2 tr, 4 ch, 2 tr) in 2ch-sp, 1 tr in next 2 tr, ch-loop, tr in next tr; rep from * twice more, tr in same 2ch-sp as first 7 ch, sl st into 3rd ch.

Round 3: Join yarn C in any 4 ch-sp, (7 ch, 2 tr) in same 4ch-sp, tr in next 4 tr, ch-loop, 1 tr in next 3 tr, *(2 tr, 4 ch, 2 tr) in 4ch-sp, 1 tr in next 4 tr, ch-loop, 1 tr in next 3 tr; rep from * twice more, tr in 1st 4ch-sp, sl st into 3rd ch.

Round 4: Join yarn D in any 4ch-sp, (7 ch, 2 tr) in same 4ch-sp, tr in next 5 tr, ch-loop, 1 tr in next 5 tr, *(2 tr, 4 ch, 2 tr) in 4ch-sp, 1 tr in next 6 tr, ch-loop, 1 tr in next 5 tr; rep from * twice more, tr in 1st 4ch-sp, sl st into 3rd ch.

Round 5: Join yarn E in any 4ch-sp, 3 ch (1 tr, 4 ch, 2 tr) in 4ch-sp, 1 tr in each st to 4ch-sp, *(2 tr, 4 ch, 2 tr) in 4ch-sp, 1 tr in each st to 4ch-sp; rep from * twice more, sl st to join.

Arrange loops: insert hook from front to back in first ch loop on round 1, *pull ch loop on next round through ch loop on hook; repeat from * twice more, leaving last ch loop free for joining. Repeat on remaining 3 sides.

Round 6: Rejoin yarn E in any 4ch-sp, repeat row 5 catching the chain loops into the stitch, fasten off.

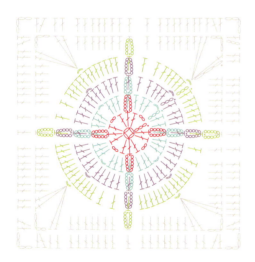

Notes
Work a chain loop (ch-loop) by doing 10 ch then sl st into the top of treble you've just made.

100 Essential Crochet Motifs

Motif 36:
She Sells Seashells on the Sea Shore

This square uses the classic shell stitch in an infinity round – keep going to create a really large square.

Yarn A
130 Old Lace

Yarn C
403 Lemonade

Yarn B
264 Light Coral

Yarn D
208 Yellow Gold

Turn after each round.
Using yarn A, 4 ch, sl st to first st to form a ring.
Round 1: 4 ch (counts as 1 tr, 1 ch), (1 tr, 1 ch) 7 times into ring, sl st to join.
Round 2: Join yarn B in any ch-sp, *1 dc in ch-sp, 6 tr in next ch-sp; rep from * 3 times, sl st to join.
Round 3: Join yarn A in any dc from the previous round, 4 ch, (1 tr, 3 ch, 1 tr, 1 ch, 1 tr, 5 ch) into the same dc, *(1 tr, 1 ch, 1 tr, 3 ch, 1 tr, 1 ch, 1 tr, 5 ch) into the next dc; rep from * twice more, sl st into top of 3rd ch of first 4 ch.
Round 4: Join yarn C in any 3ch-sp with 1 dc, 6 tr in next ch-sp, *1 dc in 5ch-sp, 6 tr in next ch-sp, 1 dc in 3ch-sp, 6 tr in next ch-sp; rep from * twice more, 1 dc in 5ch-sp, 6 tr in next ch-sp, sl st into top of first 1 dc, fasten off.
Round 5: Join A in top of the last dc worked in round 4, 4 ch, (1 tr, 3 ch, 1 tr, 1 ch, 1 tr, 5 ch), miss 6 tr, (1 tr, 1 ch, 1 tr) in next dc, 5 ch, *miss 6 tr, (1 tr, 1 ch, 1 tr, 3 ch, 1 tr, 1 ch, 1 tr, 5 ch) in next dc, miss 6 tr, (1 tr, 1 ch, 1 tr) in next dc, 5 ch; rep from * twice more, sl st to join.
Round 6: Join yarn D in any corner 3ch-sp with 1 dc, 6 tr in next ch-sp, 1 dc in next 5ch-sp, 6 tr in next ch-sp, 1 dc in next 5ch-sp, 6 tr in next ch-sp, *1 dc in next corner 3ch-sp, 6 tr in next ch-sp, 1 dc in next 5ch-sp, 6 tr in next ch-sp, 1 dc in next 5ch-sp, 6 tr in next ch-sp; rep from*twice more, sl st to join in top of first dc.
Round 7: Join yarn A in top of the last dc worked in round 6, 4 ch, (1 tr, 3 ch, 1 tr, 1 ch, 1 tr, 5 ch), miss 6 tr, (1 tr, 1 ch, 1 tr, 5 ch) in next dc twice, *(1 tr, 1 ch, 1 tr, 3 ch, 1 tr, 1 ch, 1 tr, 5 ch), miss 6 tr, (1 tr, 1 ch, 1 tr, 5 ch) in next dc twice; rep from * twice more, sl st to join. Fasten off.

Motif 37:
Groovy Baby

This striking square has retro wallpaper vibes and will take you straight back to the 1970s.

Yarn A
522 Primrose

Yarn B
524 Apricot

Yarn C
386 Peach

Yarn D
114 Shocking Pink

Yarn E
261 Capri Blue

Using yarn A, 6 ch, sl st to first st to form a ring.

Round 1: 3 ch (counts as 1 tr), 3 tr in ring, 2 ch (4 tr, 2 ch) into ring 3 times, sl st to join, fasten off, turn.

Round 2: Join yarn B in any 2ch-sp, 3 ch (2 tr, 2 ch, 3 tr) in 2ch-sp, (miss next tr, tr in space before next tr) 3 times, *(3 tr, 2 ch, 3 tr) in next 2ch-sp, (miss next tr, tr in space before next tr) 3 times; rep from * twice more, join with a sl st into the first tr, fasten off, turn.

Round 3: Join yarn C in any corner 2ch-sp, 4 ch (counts as 1 dtr), (4 dtr, 2 ch, 5 dtr) in same 2ch-sp, miss next 2 tr, 1 dc in next 5 sts, *(5 dtr, 2 ch, 5 dtr) in next 2ch-sp, miss next 2 tr, 1 dc in next 5 sts; rep from * twice more, sl st to join, turn, fasten off.

Round 4: Join yarn D in any corner 2ch-sp, 2 ch (counts as 1 htr), (2 htr, 2 ch, 3 htr) in same space, *1 htr in next 2 dtr, 1 tr in next 3 dtr, 1 dtr in next 2 dc, miss next dc, 1 dtr in next 2 dc, 1 tr in next 3 dtr, 1 htr, in next 2 dtr, (3 htr, 2 ch, 3 htr) in next corner; rep from * twice more, 1 htr in next 2 dtr, 1 tr in next 3 dtr, 1 dtr in next 2 dc, miss next dc, 1 dtr in next 2 dc, 1 tr in next 3 dtr, 1 htr, in next 2 dtr, sl st to join. Fasten off. Join in yarn E on any tr.

Round 5: 3 ch, counts as 1 tr, *1 tr in each st to corner 2ch-sp, (2 tr, 2 ch, 2 tr) in corner 2ch-sp; rep from * 3 times, 1 tr in each of last sts, sl st to join. Fasten off.

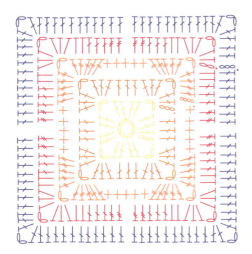

Motif 38:
Happy Flower

This bold 3D flower can't help but make you smile: it's bright and cheerful and full of fun.

Yarn A
281 Tangerine

Yarn B
208 Yellow Gold

Yarn C
222 Tulip

Using yarn A, 4 ch, sl st to first ch to form a ring.
Round 1: 3 ch (counts as first tr), 1 tr in ring, (2 ch, 2 tr) 7 times in ring, 2 ch, sl st to top of 3 ch to join, turn. Fasten off. Join yarn B in any 2ch-sp.
Round 2: 1 ch (does not count as a st), *(1 dc, 6 ch, 1 dc, 2 ch) in each 2ch-sp around, sl st to beg dc, do not turn.
Round 3: Sl st into 6 ch-sp, *(1 dc, 2 htr, 3 tr, 2 ch, 3 tr, 2 htr, 1 dc) in 6 ch-sp, 1 dc in 2ch-sp; rep from * 7 times, sl st into beg dc, turn.
Round 4: Work with wrong side facing, working in front of the petals from round 3.
Join yarn C in any dc between petals, 1 ch (1 dc in dc, 3 ch, miss next 12 sts) 8 times, sl st to beg dc, turn.
Round 5: Sl st into 3ch-sp, (3 ch, 2 tr, 3 ch 3 tr) into 3ch-sp, 1 ch, (3 tr, 1 ch) in next ch-sp, *(3 tr, 3 ch, 3 tr, 1 ch) in next 3ch-sp, (3 tr, 1 ch) in next ch-sp, (3 tr, 1 ch) in next ch-sp; rep from * twice more, sl st into top of 3 ch.
Round 6: Sl st into next ch-sp, 3 ch, (2 tr, 3 ch, 3 tr) in same sp, *(1 ch, 3 tr) in each 1 ch-sp across to next corner, *(3 tr, 3 ch, 3 tr) in corner 3ch-sp, *(1 ch, 3 tr) in each 1 ch-sp across to next corner; rep from * twice more, sl st to join, turn.
Round 7: Sl st to space between tr, *(1 ch, 3 tr) in each 1 ch-sp, (3 tr, 3 ch, 3 tr) in corner 3ch-sp; rep from * 3 times, (1 ch, 3 tr) in remaining sps between tr, sl st to join.
Round 8: *1 dc in each tr (not ch-sp) to corner, (1 dc, 2 ch, 1 dc) in corner; rep from * 3 times, 1 dc in remaining tr, sl st to join. Fasten off.

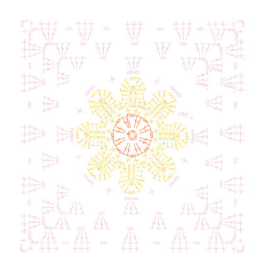

Motif 39:
Bobbling Along Square

This square uses bobble stitches to create its gorgeous texture.

Yarn A
388 Rust

Yarn B
410 Rich Coral

Yarn C
130 Old Lace

Do not turn work throughout.

Using yarn A, 4 ch, sl st to first st to form a ring.

Round 1: 3 ch (counts as 1 tr), 2 tr into ring, 2 ch, (3 tr into ring, 2 ch) 3 times, sl st to join.

Round 2: 3 ch (counts as 1 tr), 1 bobble, 1 tr, (2 tr, 2 ch, 2 tr) into 2ch-sp, *1 tr, 1 bobble, 1 tr, (2 tr, 2 ch, 2 tr) into 2ch-sp; rep from * twice more, sl st to join.

Round 3: Join yarn C in last st, 3 ch, *1 tr in each st to corner 2ch-sp, (2 tr, 2 ch, 2 tr) in 2ch-sp; rep from * 3 times, 1 tr in each of the remaining sts, sl st to join.

Round 4: 3 ch, 1 bobble, 1 tr in next 3 tr, 1 bobble, 1 tr in next tr, *(2 tr, 2 ch, 2 tr) in corner 2ch-sp, 1 tr, 1 bobble, 1 tr in next 3 tr, 1 bobble, 1 tr in next 3 tr, 1 bobble, 1 tr; rep from * twice more, 1 tr, 1 bobble, 2 tr, sl st to join.

Round 5: Join yarn C in any corner 2ch-sp, (3 ch, 1 tr, 2 ch, 2 tr) in corner 2ch-sp, 1 tr in each st to corner 2ch-sp, *(2 tr, 2 ch, 2 tr) in corner 2ch-sp, 1 tr in each st to corner space; rep from * twice more, sl st to join. Fasten off.

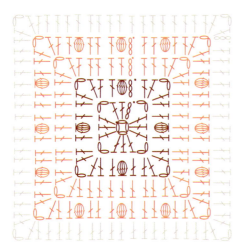

Notes
This motif uses bobble stitch. For instructions, see page 20.

Motif 40:
Gridlocked

This square in a square creates its stunning grid effect with rows of chain stitches.

Yarn A ■
110 Jet Black

Yarn C
130 Old Lace

Yarn B
519 Freesia

Using yarn A, ch 20.
Centre Grid
Row 1: 1 tr in 8th ch from hook, * 2 ch, miss 2 ch, 1 tr in next ch; rep from * 3 times.
Rows 2-5: 5 ch (counts as 1 tr, 2 ch), miss next 2 ch, (1 tr, 2 ch) into each of next 4 tr, tr in top of 3rd ch of starting 5 ch, turn.
Fasten off.

Round 1: Join yarn B in any corner space of square, 3 ch (3 tr, 2 ch 4 tr) in corner space, 2 tr in each 2ch-sp to corner space, *(4 tr, 2 ch, 4 tr) in corner space, 2 tr in each 2ch-sp to corner space; rep from * twice more, sl st to join. Fasten off, turn.
Round 2: Join yarn C in any corner 2ch-sp with a dc, *4 ch, miss 4 tr, 1 dc, 9 ch, miss 6 tr, 1 dc, 4 ch, 1 dc in corner space; rep from * 3 times replacing last dc with a sl st into first dc, turn.
Round 3: *3 ch, (6 tr, 2 ch, 6 tr) in 9ch-sp, 3 ch, 1 dc in top of next corner; rep from * 3 times, 1 dc in last corner, sl st to join, turn.
Round 4: 3 dc in next 3ch-sp, 1 dc in each tr to corner, (1 dc, 2 ch, 1 dc) in corner, *1 dc in each tr, 3 dc in next 3ch-sp, 1 dc in next dc, 3 dc in next 3ch-sp, 1 dc in each tr to corner, (1 dc, 2 ch, 1 dc) in corner; rep from * twice more, 1 dc in each tr, 3 dc in next 3ch-sp, 1 dc in next dc, sl st to join, fasten off.

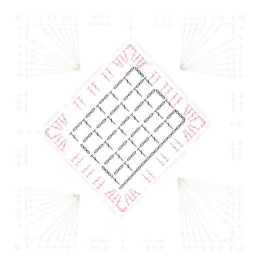

100 Essential Crochet Motifs

Motif 41:
In Full Bloom

This beautiful square reminds me of a brilliant blue flower and all its foliage.

Yarn A
403 Lemonade

Yarn B
414 Vintage Peach

Yarn C
397 Cyan

Yarn D
513 Apple Granny

Yarn E
130 Old Lace

Using yarn A, 6 ch, sl st to first st to form a ring.
Round 1: 3 ch (counts as 1 tr), 15 tr in ring, sl st to top of beg 3 ch to join, turn.
Fasten off. Join yarn B in any st.
Round 2: 2 ch, 1 tr in same st (counts as tr2tog), 1 ch, tr2tog in next st, 2 ch, *tr2tog in next st, 1 ch, tr2tog in next st, 2 ch; rep from * around, sl st to join, turn.
Fasten off. Join yarn C in any ch-sp.
Round 3: *2 ch, (tr3tog, 1 ch, tr3tog) in 2ch-sp, 2 ch, 1 dc in 1 ch-sp; rep from * around, sl st to join, turn.
Fasten off. Join yarn D in any dc.
Round 4: 3 ch, (1 tr, 2 ch, 2 tr) in same dc, 4 ch, 1 htr in next dc, 4 ch, *(2 tr, 2 ch, 2 tr) in next dc, 4 ch, 1 htr in next dc, 4 ch; rep from * twice more, sl st to join, turn.
Fasten off. Join yarn E in any corner 2ch-sp.
Round 5: 3 ch, (1 tr, 2 ch, 2 tr) in same 2ch-sp, 2 tr, (4 tr in next 4 ch-sp) twice, 2 tr, *(2 tr, 2 ch, 2 tr) in corner 2ch-sp, 2 tr, (4 tr in next 4 ch-sp) twice, 2 tr; rep from * twice more, sl st to join. Fasten off.

Motif 42:
Flower Chain Square

The delicate chain detail at the centre of this square resembles pretty little petals.

Yarn A
520 Lavender

Yarn C
189 Royal Orange

Yarn B
252 Watermelon

Yarn D
282 Ultra Violet

Do not turn work throughout.
Using yarn A, 6 ch, sl st to first ch to form a ring.
Round 1: Sl st into ring (11 ch, sl st into ring) 12 times. Fasten off.
Round 2: Join yarn B in any 11ch-sp with a dc, *6 ch, dc into next 11ch-sp, (4 ch, dc in next 11ch-sp) twice; rep from * 3 times, sl st to beg dc.
Round 3: Sl st into 6ch-sp, 4 ch (counts as 1 dtr), (2 dtr, 2 ch, 3 dtr) in same 6ch-sp, 3 tr in next 2 4ch-sp, *(3 dtr, 2 ch, 3 dtr) in next 6ch-sp, 3 tr in next 2 4ch-sp; rep from * twice more, sl st into top of 4 ch to join. Fasten off.
Round 4: Join yarn C in any corner 2ch-sp, *(1 dc, 2 ch, 1 dc) in same corner space, (3 ch, miss 3 sts, 1 dc in space between 3 sts) 3 times, 3 ch; rep from * 3 times, sl st to join. Fasten off.
Round 5: Join yarn D in any corner 2ch-sp, *(1 dc, 2 ch, 1 dc), 3 dc in each 3ch-sp to corner; rep from * 3 times, sl st to join. Fasten off.

Motif 43:
V-stitch Square

This V-stitch square is nice and airy. It can be made in one colour or you can switch colours each row.

Yarn A
414 Vintage Peach

Yarn B
512 Lime

Yarn C
519 Freesia

Yarn D
280 Lemon

Yarn E
100 Lemon Chiffon

Turn after each round.
Using yarn A, 4 ch, sl st to first st to form a ring.
Round 1: 4 ch (counts as 1 tr, 1 ch), 1 tr into ring, 2 ch, *(1 v-st, 2 ch) into ring 3 times , sl st to join. Fasten off, turn.
Round 2: Join yarn B in corner 2ch-sp, 4 ch (counts as 1 tr, 1 ch), (1 tr, 2 ch, 1 v-st) in same space, 1 v-st in ch-sp of v-stitch from previous round, *(1 v-st, 2 ch, 1 v-st) in 2ch-sp, 1 v-st in ch-sp of v-stitch from previous round; rep from * twice more, sl st to join. Fasten off, turn.
Round 3: Join yarn C in corner 2ch-sp, 4 ch (counts as 1 tr, 1 ch), (1 tr, 2 ch, 1 v-stitch) in same space, 1 v-stitch in each ch-sp of v-stitch from previous round to corner, *(1 v-stitch, 2 ch, 1 v-stitch) in 2ch-sp, 1 v-stitch in each ch-sp of v-stitch to corner; rep from * twice more, sl st to join. Fasten off, turn.
Round 4: Rep round 3 using yarn D. Fasten off.
Round 5: Rep round 3 using yarn E. Fasten off.

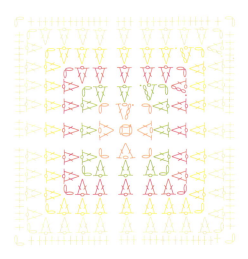

Notes
V-stitch (v-st) is 1 treble, 1 chain, 1 treble (1 tr, 1 ch, 1 tr) worked into the same chain space or stitch.

Motif 44:
Spiral Swirl

This spiral square is easier than it looks. You can work it using two or four colours.

Yarn A
130 Old Lace

Yarn C
524 Apricot

Yarn B
519 Freesia

Yarn D
164 Light Navy

Do not turn work throughout.
Using yarn A, 4 ch, sl st to first st to form a ring.
Round 1: *1 dc, 1 htr, 2 tr into centre of ring, pull up a long loop, remove hook **;
Join yarn B with a sl st; rep from * to **,
Join yarn C with a sl st; rep from * to **,
Join yarn D with a sl st; rep from * to **.
You should now have the same number of sts in each colour in 4 separate sections.
Round 2: Pick up yarn A, * 2 tr in next st (working into yarn B) 1 tr in next st, 2 tr in next st, leave last st unworked, leave a long loop, remove hook **;
repeat from * to ** for B, C, and D.
Round 3: Pick up yarn A, *2 tr in next st, 1 tr in next 3 sts, 2 tr in next st, leave last st unworked, leave a long loop, remove hook **; repeat from * to ** for B, C and D.
Round 4: Pick up yarn A, *2 tr in next st, 1 tr in next 5 sts, 2 tr in next st, leave last st unworked, leave a long loop, remove hook **; rep from * to ** for B, C and D.
Round 5: Pick up yarn A, *2 tr in next st, 1 tr in next 7 sts, 2 tr in next st, leave last st unworked, leave a long loop, remove hook **; rep from * to ** for B, C and D.
Round 6: Pick up yarn A, *2 tr in next st, 1 tr in next 9 sts, 2 tr in next st, leave last st unworked, leave a long loop, remove hook **; rep from * to * for B, C and D.
Round 7: Return to yarn A, *(2 tr, 2 ch, 2 tr) in next st, 1 tr in next st, 1 htr in next st, 1 dc in next st, 1 sl st in next 2 sts, fasten off **; rep from * to ** for B, C and D.
Round 8: Join Yarn A in any corner 2ch-sp, (1 dc, 2 ch, 1 dc) in corner space, 1 dc in each st to corner 2ch-sp; rep from * 3 times, sl st to join. Fasten off.

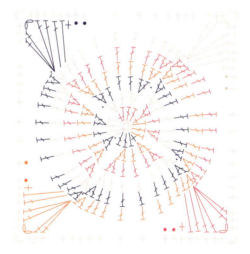

Motif 45:
Sidari Square

This fun motif uses a great combination of stitches to make this quirky square.

Yarn A
256 Cornelia Rose

Yarn C
105 Bridal White

Yarn B
146 Vivid Blue

Yarn D
114 Shocking Pink

Turn after each round.

Using yarn A, 6 ch, sl st to first st to form a ring.

Round 1: 3 ch (counts as 1 tr), 15 tr into 6 ch loop, sl st to join, turn. Fasten off.

Round 2: Join yarn B in between any 2 tr stitches, 2 tr in space between trs, 1 ch, work (2 tr, 1 ch) in each space between trs around, sl st to join, turn. Fasten off.

Round 3: Join yarn C in any ch-sp, (3 ch, 2 tr, 1 ch) in same ch-sp, work (3 tr, 1 ch) in each ch-sp around, sl st to join, turn. Fasten off.

Round 4: Join yarn D in any ch-sp, *(6 ch, 1 dc) in same ch-sp, (4 ch, 1 dc) in next ch-sp 4 times; rep from * 3 times, sl st to join, turn. Don't fasten off.

Round 5: Sl st into 4ch-sp, *1 dc in 4ch-sp, (4 tr, 1 ch) in next 4ch-sp, 4 tr in next 4ch-sp, 1 dc in next 4 ch-sp, (5 tr, 2 ch, 5 tr) in 6ch-sp; rep from * 3 times, sl st into first dc to join. Fasten off.

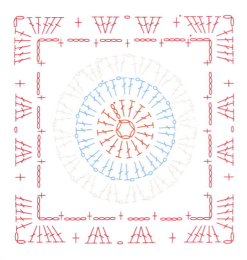

70   100 Essential Crochet Motifs

Motif 46:
Alexis Square

These colourful motifs are worked along two sides only, then joined together with dc edging.

Yarn A
189 Royal Orange

Yarn C
400 Petrol Blue

Yarn B
114 Shocking Pink

Yarn D
130 Old Lace

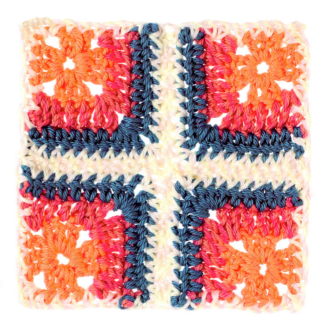

Turn after each round.
Using yarn A, 4 ch, sl st to first st to form a ring.
Make 4
Round 1: (3 ch, 2 tr, 2 ch) into ring, *(3 tr, 2 ch) into ring; repeat from * twice more.
Round 2: Join yarn B in any 2ch-sp and work along 2 sides of the square only for the remaining rounds.
(3 ch, 1 tr) in same 2ch-sp, 1 tr in each tr, (2 tr, 2 ch, 2 tr) in corner space, 1 tr in each of next 3 tr and 2 tr in corner space. Fasten off.
Round 3: Join yarn C in last st of last row, 2 ch (counts as 1 htr), 1 htr in each tr to 2ch-sp, (2 htr, 2 ch, 2 htr) in corner space, 1 htr in each tr to end. Fasten off.
Round 4: Join yarn D in last st from previous round, 1 dc in each htr to corner, (1 dc, 2 ch, 1 dc) in corner 2ch-sp, 1 dc in each htr to end. Fasten off.

Arrange as shown in image, join using yarn D using a neat whip stitch on the wrong side.

Round 5: Using yarn D work 1 row dc around entire square, *(1 dc, 2 ch, 1 dc) in corner, work 1 dc in each top of tr, corner space, side of htr and side of dc, and 2 dc in side of tr to corner; rep from * 3 times, sl st to join. Fasten off.

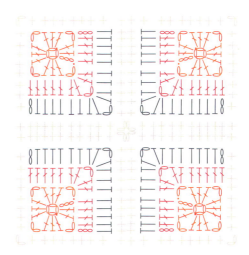

Notes
For whip-stitch instructions, see page 21.

Motif 47:
Catherine Wheel

This lovely openwork square uses double trebles to create the spokes of the Catherine wheel.

Yarn A
281 Tangerine

Yarn C
256 Cornelia Rose

Yarn B
130 Old Lace

Yarn D
511 Cornflower

Turn after each round.
Using yarn A, 6 ch, sl st to first st to form a ring.
Round 1: 1 ch (doesn't count as a stitch), 16 dc into ring, sl st to join. Fasten off.
Round 2: Join yarn B to any dc, 5 ch (counts as 1 dtr, 1 ch) in dc, (1 dtr, 1 ch) in each st around, sl st into top of 4 ch, fasten off, turn.
Round 3: Join Yarn C in any 1 ch-sp, 3 dc, 1 ch in each 1 ch-space around, sl st to join, turn.
Round 4: Sl st into 1 ch-sp, *1 dc in 1 ch-sp, miss 3 dc, (5 tr, 2 ch, 5 tr) in next 1 ch-sp, miss 3 dc; rep from * 7 times, sl st into top of first dc to join, fasten off, turn.
Round 5: Join yarn B in any 2ch-sp with 1 dc, *5 ch, miss 5 tr, 1 dc in top of dc, miss 5 tr 1 dc in 2ch-sp; rep around, finish with 5 ch and sl st into top of first dc in 2ch-sp, turn, do not fasten off.
Round 6: Join yarn D in same place as last sl st, 4 ch (counts as 1 dtr), (3 dtr, 3 ch, 4 dtr) in top of dc made in the 2ch-space in the previous round, 6 ch, 1 dc in dc made in the top of 2ch-space from previous round, 6 ch, *(4 dtr, 3 ch, 4 dtr) in top of dc made in the 2ch-space in the previous round, 6 ch, 1 dc in dc made in the top of 2ch-space from previous round, 6 ch; rep from * twice more, sl st into top of first 4 ch to join, fasten off.

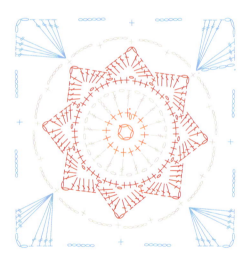

100 Essential Crochet Motifs

Motif 48:
Little Pearl Square

This motif uses overlapping treble togethers for a raised texture that contrasts with the open chains.

Yarn A
516 Candy Apple

Yarn B
251 Garden Rose

Yarn C
246 Icy Pink

Yarn D
130 Old Lace

Do not turn work throughout.
Using yarn A, 4 ch, sl st to first st to form a ring.
Round 1: 1 ch (doesn't count as a stitch), 12 dc into ring, sl st to join.
Round 2: *7 ch, miss 3 dc, 1 dc in next dc; rep from * twice more, 7 ch, sl st into first st. Fasten off.
Round 3: Join yarn B in any 7ch-sp, [3 ch (counts as 1 tr), 8 tr) in same 7ch-sp, 3 ch, * 9 tr in next 7 ch-sp, 3 ch; rep from * twice more, sl st to join.
Round 4: 3 ch (counts as 1st tr of tr3tog), tr2tog, (3 ch, tr3tog starting in last st of previous tr3tog) 3 times, 6 ch, 1 dtr in 3ch-sp, 6 ch, * tr3tog, (3 ch, tr3tog starting in last st of previous tr3tog) 3 times, 6 ch, 1 dtr in 3ch-sp, 6 ch; repeat from * twice more, sl st into top of first tr3tog. Fasten off.
Round 5: Join yarn C in the top of any dtr, 3 ch, (2 tr, 2 ch, 3 tr) in same dtr, 3 tr in 6ch-sp, 3 tr in next 3 3ch-sps, 3 tr in next 6ch-sp, *(3 tr, 2 ch, 3 tr) in same dtr, 3 tr in 6 ch-sp, 3 tr in next 3 3ch-sps, 3 tr in next 6ch-sp; rep from * twice more, sl st to join.
Round 6: Join yarn D in any corner space, 3 ch, (1 tr, 2 ch, 2 tr) in corner space, 1 tr in each tr to corner space, *(2 tr, 2 ch, 2 tr) in corner space, 1 tr in each tr to corner space; rep from * twice more, sl st to join. Fasten off.

100 Essential Crochet Motifs

Motif 49:
Orla Square

The central design of this small square looks particularly striking with the pale lace around it.

Yarn A ■
400 Petrol Blue

Yarn C ▫
130 Old Lace

Yarn B ■
514 Jade

Turn after each round.
Using yarn A, 6 ch, sl st to first st to form a ring.
Round 1: 3 ch (counts as 1 tr), 15 tr into ring, sl st to join. Fasten off.
Round 2: Join yarn B in any tr with *1 dc, 1 ch, miss 1 tr, 7 tr in next st, miss 1 tr, 1 ch; rep from * 3 times, sl st to join. Fasten off, turn.
Round 3: Join yarn C in any dc from previous round, (4 ch, 1 dtr, 4 ch, 2 dtr) in same dc, 2 ch, miss 3 tr, 1 dc in top of 4th tr of 7 tr, 2 ch, miss 3 tr, *(2 dtr, 4 ch, 2 dtr) in same dc, 2 ch, miss 3 tr, 1 dc in top of 4th tr of 7 tr, 2 ch, miss 3 tr; rep from * twice more, sl st to join.
Round 4: Sl st into 2ch-sp, 3 ch, 1 tr in 2ch-sp, 1 tr in top of dc, 2 tr in 2ch-sp, 1 tr in top of next 2 dtr, (2 tr, 2 ch, 2 tr) in corner space, 1 tr in top of next 2 dtr, *2 tr in 2ch-sp, 1 tr in top of dc, 2 tr in 2ch-sp, 1 tr in top of next 2 dtr, (2 tr, 2 ch, 2 tr) in corner space, 1 tr in next 2 dtr; rep from * twice more, sl st to join. Fasten off.

Motif 50:
Purple Twist

V-stitches, treble togethers and multiple trebles in combination make this easier than it looks.

Yarn A
256 Cornelia Rose

Yarn B
519 Freesia

Yarn C
520 Lavender

Yarn D
514 Jade

Yarn E
113 Delphinium

Turn after each round.
Using yarn A, 6 ch, sl st to first st to form a ring.
Round 1: 3 ch (counts as 1 tr), 15 tr into ring, sl st to join. Fasten off.
Round 2: Join yarn B in any tr, 4 ch (counts as 1 tr, 1 ch), 1 tr in same st, *miss 1 tr, 1 v-stitch in next st; rep from * 6 times, miss 1 tr, sl st to join, fasten off.
Round 3: Join yarn C in any ch-sp, 3 ch (counts as first tr of tr5tog), tr4tog, 5 ch, *tr5tog in next ch-sp, 5 ch; rep from * 6 times, sl st to join.
Round 4: Join yarn D in any 5ch-sp, 3 ch (counts as 1 tr), 7 tr in same 5ch-sp, 8 tr in each of next 7 5ch-sp, sl st to join.
Round 5: Sl st into space between 2 sets of 8 tr, 3 ch, (2 tr, 2 ch, 3 tr) in same space, miss 3 tr, 1 dc in next 10 tr, miss 3 tr, *(3 tr, 2 ch, 3 tr) in next space, miss 3 tr, 1 dc in next 10 tr, miss 3 tr; rep from * twice more, sl st to join. Fasten off.
Round 6: Join yarn E in any corner 2ch-sp, (2 ch, 1 htr, 2 ch, 2 htr) in corner 2ch-sp, 1 htr in each st to corner space, *(2 htr, 2 ch, 2 htr) in corner space, 1 htr in each st to corner space; rep from * twice more, sl st to join. Fasten off.

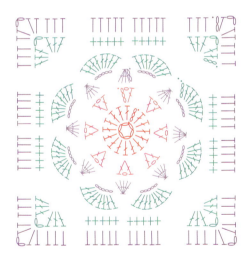

Notes
V-stitch (v-st) is 1 treble, 1 chain, 1 treble (1 tr, 1 ch, 1 tr) worked into the same chain space or stitch. For treble togethers (in this case, tr5tog), see instructions on pages 14 and 15.

100 Essential Crochet Motifs

Motif 51:
Granny Hexagon

For this first hexagon, sets of two trebles make for a lovely lattice-work effect.

Yarn A ▪
520 Lavender

Yarn B ▪
524 Apricot

Yarn C ▪
282 Ultra Violet

Yarn D ▪
114 Shocking Pink

Yarn E ▪
130 Old Lace

Turn after each round.
Using yarn A, 4 ch, sl st to first st to form a ring.
Round 1: (3 ch, 1 tr, 2 ch) into ring, *(2 tr, 2 ch) into ring; repeat from * 4 times. Fasten off.
Round 2: Join yarn B in any 2ch-sp, 3 ch, (1 tr, 2 ch, 2 tr) in same 2ch-sp, (2 tr, 2 ch, 2 tr) in each 2ch-sp around, sl st to join. Fasten off.
Round 3: Join yarn C in any 2ch-sp, 3 ch, (1 tr, 2 ch, 2 tr) in same 2ch-sp, 2 tr in space between sets of 2 tr, *(2 tr, 2 ch, 2 tr) in next 2ch-sp, 2 tr in space between sets of 2 tr; rep from * 4 times, sl st to join. Fasten off.
Round 4: Join yarn D in any 2ch-sp, 3 ch, (1 tr, 2 ch, 2 tr) in same 2ch-sp, 2 tr in each sp between sets of 2 tr, *(2 tr, 2 ch, 2 tr) in next 2ch-sp, 2 tr in each sp between sets of 2 tr; rep from * 4 times, sl st to join. Fasten off.
Round 5: Rep round 4 using yarn E.

100 Essential Crochet Motifs

Motif 52:
Peaceful Hexagon

This hexagon, in lovely calming shades, can be as big as you want – just keep repeating round 3!

Yarn A
201 Electric Blue

Yarn B
513 Apple Granny

Yarn C
397 Cyan

Yarn D
208 Yellow Gold

Yarn E
130 Old Lace

Using yarn A, 6 ch, sl st to form a ring.

Round 1: 3 ch (counts as 1 tr), 1 tr into ring, 2 ch, (2 tr, 2 ch) into ring 5 times, sl st to 3rd of beg 3 ch to join. Turn. Fasten off.

Round 2: Join yarn B in any 2ch-sp, (3 ch, 2 ch, 1 tr) in first 2ch-sp, 1 tr in each tr to next corner 2ch-sp, *(1 tr, 2 ch, 1 tr) in 2ch-sp, 1 tr in each tr to next 2ch-sp; rep from * around, sl st to 3rd of beg 3 ch to join. Turn. Fasten off.

Round 3: Join yarn C in any corner 2ch-sp, (3 ch, 2 ch, 1 tr) in corner 2ch-sp, 1 tr in each tr to corner 2ch-sp, *(1 tr, 2 ch, 1 tr) in 2ch-sp, 1 tr in each tr to corner 2ch-sp; rep from * 4 times, sl st to 3rd of beg 3 ch to join. Turn. Fasten off.

Round 4: Rep round 3 using yarn D.

Round 5: Rep round 3 using yarn E.

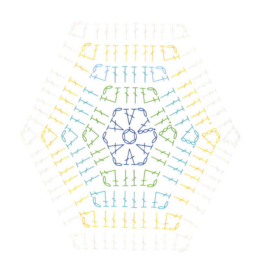

100 Essential Crochet Motifs

Motif 53:
Daisy Hexagon

Double treble clusters add texture to this pretty daisy motif with its central spokes of single treble stitches.

Yarn A
208 Yellow Gold

Yarn C
252 Watermelon

Yarn B
130 Old Lace

Using yarn A, 6 ch, sl st to first ch to form a ring.
Round 1: 4 ch (counts as 1 tr and 1 ch), (1 tr, 1 ch) 11 times in ring, sl st to 3rd of beg 4 ch to join, turn. Fasten off yarn A.
Join yarn B in any ch-sp.
Round 2: BegDtr3Cl in first ch-sp, *3 ch, 1 Dtr3Cl in next ch-sp; rep from * around, 3 ch, sl st to top of BegDtr3Cl to join, turn. Fasten off yarn B.
Join yarn C in any 3ch-sp.
Round 3: 4 ch, (2 dtr, 2 ch, 3 dtr) in same 3ch-sp, *3 dtr in next 3ch-sp, (3 dtr, 2 ch, 3 dtr) in next 3ch-sp; rep from * 4 times, 3 dtr in next 3ch-sp, sl st to top of beg 3 ch to join. Fasten off.

Notes
This uses clusters of 3 double treble stitches (Dtr3Cl) and beginning clusters with 4 chain stitches making the first double treble stitch (BegDtr3Cl). For Cluster instructions, see page 16.

Motif 54:
Matisse Hexagon

The colours of this hexagon remind me of the joyous tones of Henri Matisse's paintings.

Yarn A
389 Apple Green

Yarn B
130 Old Lace

Yarn C
513 Apple Granny

Yarn D
511 Cornflower

Yarn E
261 Capri Blue

Turn after each round.
Using yarn A, 3 ch, sl st to form a ring.
Round 1: (3 ch, 1 tr) in ring (counts as 1 tr2Cl), (3 ch, 1 tr2Cl) 5 times in ring, 3 ch, sl st to top of 3 ch to join. Fasten off, turn.
Round 2: Join yarn B in any 3ch-sp, 3 ch (counts as 1 tr), 4 tr in same 3ch-sp, 5 tr in each of next 5 3ch-sps, sl st to 3 ch to join. Fasten off, turn.
Round 3: Join yarn C in any sp between 5 tr groups, 3 ch, 4 tr in same sp, miss 2 sts, 1 v-st in next st, miss 2 tr, *5 tr in space between 5 tr grps, miss 2 sts, 1 v-st in next st, miss 2 tr; rep from * around, sl st to top of 3 ch to join. Fasten off, turn.
Round 4: Join yarn D in any ch-sp of v-st, 4 ch (counts as 1 tr, 1 ch), 1 tr in same ch-sp, 1 ch, miss 2nd tr of v-st, 5 tr, 1 ch, *1 v-st in ch-sp of next v-st, 1 ch, miss 2nd tr of v-st, 5 tr, 1 ch; rep from * around, sl st to 3rd ch of beg 4 ch to join. Fasten off, turn.
Round 5: Join yarn E in any ch-sp of v-stitch, (4 ch, 1 tr) in same ch-sp, 1 ch, 1 tr in ch-sp, 5 tr, 1 tr in ch-sp, 1 ch, *1 v-st in ch-sp of next v-st, 1 ch, 1 tr in ch-sp, 5 tr, 1 tr in ch-sp, 1 ch; rep from * around, sl st to join. Fasten off.

Notes
This uses a variation of Cluster stitch with 2 treble stitches (tr2Cl). For Cluster instructions, see page 16.

The open design is partly created with V stitches (v-st), which are simply 1 treble, 1 chain, 1 treble (1 tr, 1 ch, 1 tr) in the same stitch.

100 Essential Crochet Motifs

Motif 55:
African Violet Hexagon

I love designing these flowers in all shapes and sizes, like this gorgeous hexagon.

Yarn A ■
110 Jet Black

Yarn C ■
281 Tangerine

Yarn B ■
519 Freesia

Yarn D ■
130 Old Lace

Using yarn A, 4 ch, sl st to form a ring.

Round 1: 3 ch (counts as 1 tr), 1 tr in ring, 1 ch, (2 tr, 1 ch) in ring 5 times, sl st to top of beg 3 ch to join, turn. Fasten off yarn A, join yarn B in any ch-sp.

Round 2: (3 ch, 2 tr) in same ch-sp, 2 ch, (3 tr, 2 ch) in each ch-sp around, sl st to top of beg 3 ch to join, turn. Fasten off, join yarn C in any 2ch-sp.

Round 3: (3 ch, 1 tr, 3 ch, 2 tr, 1 ch) in same 2ch-sp, (2 tr, 3 ch, 2 tr, 1 ch) in each 2ch-sp around, sl st to top of beg 3 ch to join, turn. Do not fasten off. Sl st into 3ch-sp.

Round 4: (3 ch, 6 tr, 1 ch) in same 3ch-sp, (7 tr, 1 ch) in each 3ch-sp around, sl st to top of beg 3 ch to join, turn. Fasten off, join yarn D in first tr of any 7 tr group.

Round 5: *1 dc in each of next 7 tr, 1 Sp-dc in ch-sp in round 3 below; rep from * around, sl st to first dc to join. Don't turn. Fasten off yarn D.
Join yarn A in 4th dc of any 7 dc group.

Round 6: 5 ch (counts as 1 tr and 2 ch), 1 tr in same dc, 1 tr in each of next 3 dc, 1 tr in Sp-dc, 1 tr in each of next 3 dc, *(1 tr, 2 ch, 1 tr) in next dc, 1 tr in each of next 3 dc, 1 tr in Sp-dc, 1 tr in each of next 3 dc; rep from * 4 times, sl st to 3rd of beg 4 ch to join. Fasten off.

Notes
This hexagon creates shell stitches with the 7 trebles in round 4, and uses spike double crochet stitches (Sp-dc) to outline the petals. For spike stitch instructions, see page 19.

100 Essential Crochet Motifs

Motif 56:
Wagon Wheel Hexagon

The spokes of this wagon wheel are created by crocheting together two double trebles.

Yarn A
208 Yellow Gold

Yarn B
386 Peach

Yarn C
201 Electric Blue

Yarn D
519 Freesia

Yarn E
130 Old Lace

Using yarn A and hook, 4 ch, sl st to form a ring.
Round 1: 3 ch (counts as 1 tr), 11 tr into ring, sl st to top of 3 ch to join. Fasten off. Turn.
Round 2: Join yarn B in any tr, 4 ch and 1 dtr in any tr (counts as first dtr2tog), miss 1 tr, 7 ch, (1 dtr2tog, 7 ch) 5 times, sl st into top of 4 ch to join, turn.
Round 3: Join yarn C in any dtr2tog, 3 ch 2 tr in same st, 7 tr in 7ch-sp, *3 tr in top of dtr2tog, 7 tr in 7ch-sp; rep from * 4 times, sl st to join. Fasten off.
Round 4: Join yarn D in any of the centre trs made in the top of the dtr2tog, (4 ch, 1 tr, 1 ch, 1 tr) in same st, [miss 1 tr, 1 ch, 1 tr in next st] 4 times, 1 ch, miss 1 tr *(1 tr, 1 ch, 1 tr, 1 ch, 1 tr) in centre st made in dtr2tog below, [miss 1 tr, 1 ch, 1 tr in next st] 4 times, 1 ch; rep from * 4 times, sl st to join. Fasten off.
Round 5: Join yarn E in first corner ch-sp, * work 2 dc in first ch-sp of corner, 2 ch, then 2 dc in second ch-sp in corner, work 2 dc in each ch-sp to next corner; rep from * 5 times, sl st to join. Fasten off.

Notes
The dtr2tog stitches in this hexagon combine 2 double trebles to create the spokes.

For instructions on double treble, see page 13.
For instructions on trebling together, see page 14.

100 Essential Crochet Motifs

Motif 57:
Pretty Pink Hexagon

This delicate hexagon uses treble stitches and treble cluster stitches to create the lacy effect.

Yarn A
238 Powder Pink

Turn after each round.
Using Yarn A, 4 ch, sl st to first ch to form a ring.
Round 1: 4 ch (counts as 1 tr, 1 ch), (1 tr, 1 ch) 11 times in ring, sl st in first ch-sp to join, turn.
Round 2: 6 ch (counts as 1 tr, 3 ch), (1 tr, 3 ch) in each ch-sp around, sl st in 3rd of beg 6 ch, turn.
Round 3: Sl st into 3ch-sp, 3 ch, tr2tog in same ch-sp (counts as 3trCl), *(5 ch, 3trCl) in each ch-sp around, sl st in top of 3 ch to join, turn.
Round 4: 4 ch (counts as 1 tr, 1 ch), 1 tr in top of same 3trCl, 3 ch, 1 dc in 5ch-sp, 3 ch, 1 dc in top of 3trCl, 3 ch, 1 dc in 5ch-sp, 3 ch, *(1 tr, 1 ch, 1 tr) in top of 3trCl, 3 ch, 1 dc in 5ch-sp, 3 ch, 1 dc in top of Cl, 3 ch, 1 dc in 5ch-sp, 3 ch; rep from * 4 times, sl st in top of 3 ch to join.
Fasten off.

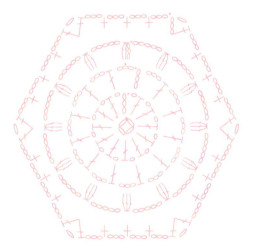

Notes
This uses clusters of 3 treble stitches (3trCl).
For Cluster instructions, see page 16.

100 Essential Crochet Motifs

Motif 58:
Starburst Hexagon

A combination of puff stitches and cluster stitches gives this hexagon a lovely texture.

Yarn A
164 Light Navy

Yarn C
173 Bluebell

Yarn B
114 Shocking Pink

Yarn D
130 Old Lace

Do not turn work throughout.
Using yarn A, 6 ch, sl st to first ch to form a ring.
Round 1: 3 ch (counts as 1 tr), 1 tr 17 times in ring, sl st in first 3 ch to join.
Round 2: Join yarn B in any tr, work 1 BegPuff in first space, 1 ch, (1 puff, 1 ch) in each st around, sl st to join.
Round 3: Join yarn C, 2 ch (counts as first st in 4trCl), tr3tog, 2 ch, (4trCl, 2 ch) in each ch-sp around, sl st to join. Fasten off.
Round 4: Join yarn D in any 2ch-sp, 3 ch (counts as 1 tr), (2 tr in same space, 2 ch, 3 tr), 3 tr in next 2 2ch-sps, *(3 tr, 2 ch, 3 tr) in next 2ch-sp, 3 tr in next 2 2ch-sps; rep from * 4 times, sl st to join. Fasten off.

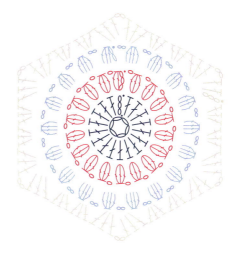

Notes
For instructions on puff and beginning puff (BegPuff) stitches (where 2 loops of the puff are replaced by 3 chain stitches), see page 17.

The motif also uses clusters of 4 treble stitches (4trCl). For instructions on cluster stitches, see page 16.

100 Essential Crochet Motifs

Motif 59:
All the Blues Hexagon

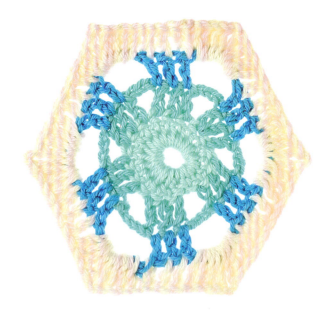

This lovely cross shape in shades of blue reminds me of an ancient stained-glass window.

Yarn A
385 Crystalline

Yarn B
253 Tropic

Yarn C
146 Vivid Blue

Yarn D
130 Old Lace

Do not turn work throughout.

Using yarn A, 6 ch, sl st to first ch to form a ring.

Round 1: 3 ch (counts as 1 tr), 17 tr in ring, sl st in first 3 ch to join, turn. Fasten off.

Round 2: Join yarn B in any tr, 3 ch (counts as 1 tr), 1 tr in next 2 sts, 3 ch, *1 tr in next 3 sts, 3 ch; rep from * 4 times, sl st to join, turn. Fasten off.

Round 3: Join Yarn C in the first tr of any of the sets of 3 stitches, 3 ch (counts as 1 tr), 1 tr in next 2 sts, 5 ch, *1 tr in next 3 sts, 5 ch; rep from * 4 times, sl st to join. Fasten off.

Round 4: Join yarn D in any 5ch-sp, 3 ch (counts as 1 tr), (3 tr, 2 ch, 4 tr) in 5ch-sp, 1 tr in each of next 3 tr, *(4 tr, 2 ch, 4 tr) in 5ch-sp, 1 tr in each of next 3 tr; rep from * 4 times, sl st to join. Fasten off.

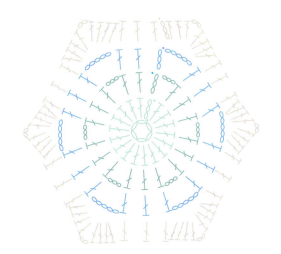

Motif 60:
Hexagon 3D Flower

The 3D effect of these petals is created by working behind the previous rounds.

Yarn A
264 Light Coral

Do not turn work throughout.
Using yarn A, 4 ch, sl st to form a ring.
Round 1: 3 ch (counts as first half of tr2tog), 1 tr, 2 ch, (1 tr2tog, 2 ch) 5 times in ring, sl st to join.
Round 2: Sl st into 2ch-sp, (1 dc, 1 ch, 5 tr, 1 ch 1 dc) in each 2ch-sp around.
Round 3: 1 ch, working behind petals made on round 2, insert hook from back to front to back, work 1 sl st behind first tr2tog of round 1, *3 ch, inserting hook from back to front to back, work 1 dc around next tr2tog; rep from * around (6 x 3ch-sps).
Round 4: Sl st in next 3ch-sp, (1 dc, 1 ch, 1 tr, 6 dtr, 1 tr, 1 ch, 1 dc) in each 3ch-sp around.
Round 5: 1 ch, working behind petals made on round 4, inserting hook from back to front to back, sl st behind next dc made on round 3, *4 ch, 1 dc around next dc on round 3; rep from * around.
Round 6: Sl st into 4ch-sp, 3 ch (counts as 1 tr), (2 tr, 2 ch, 3 tr) in same 4ch-sp, *(3 tr, 2 ch 3 tr) in each 3ch-sp around, sl st into top of first 3 ch.
Round 7: 3 ch (counts as 1 tr), *1 tr in each tr to corner space, (1 tr, 2 ch, 1 tr) in 2 ch corner space; rep from * 5 times, 1 tr in each tr, sl st to join.

Motif 61:
Circle in a Hexagon

I love the summery colours of this motif. It would look striking made into a larger project.

Yarn A
208 Yellow Gold

Yarn B
114 Shocking Pink

Yarn C
513 Apple Granny

Yarn D
130 Old Lace

Turn after each round.
Using Yarn A, 4 ch, sl st to first ch to form a ring.
Round 1: 3 ch (counts as 1 tr), 11 tr in ring, sl st in first 3 ch to join. Fasten off.
Round 2: Join yarn B in any tr, 3 ch (counts as 1 tr), 1 tr in same st, 2 tr in each of the trs around, sl st to join. Fasten off.
Round 3: Join yarn C in any tr, 3 ch (counts as 1 tr), 1 tr in same tr, 1 tr in next tr, *2 tr in next tr, 1 tr in next tr; rep from * around, sl st to join. Fasten off.
Round 4: Join yarn D in any tr, 3 ch (counts as 1 tr), (1 tr, 2 ch, 2 tr) in same tr, 1 htr in next 5 tr, *(2 tr, 2 ch, 2 tr) in next tr, 1 htr in next 5 tr; rep from * 4 times, sl st to join. Fasten off.

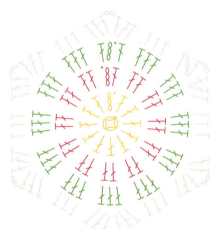

Motif 62:
Moss Stitch Hexagon

Create moss stitch crochet by working into chain spaces on the right and wrong sides of the motif.

Yarn A
253 Tropic

Yarn B
403 Lemonade

Yarn C
411 Sweet Orange

Yarn D
414 Vintage Peach

Yarn E
409 Soft Rose

Yarn F
130 Old Lace

Using yarn A, 4 ch, sl st to first ch to form a ring.
Round 1: 5 ch (counts as 1 tr, 2 ch), (1 tr, 2 ch) 5 times in ring, sl st in 3rd of first 5 ch to join, turn.
Round 2: Sl st into 2ch-sp, *(1 dc, 2 ch 1 dc, 1 ch) in each 2ch-sp around, sl st to join. Fasten off, turn.
Round 3: Join yarn B in corner 2ch-sp, *(1 dc, 2 ch, 1 dc, 1 ch) in corner space, 1 dc in ch-sp, 1 ch; rep from * 5 times, sl st to join. Fasten off, turn.
Round 4: Join yarn C in any corner 2ch-sp *(1 dc, 2 ch, 1 dc, 1 ch) in corner space, (1 dc, 1 ch) in each ch-sp to corner space; rep from * 5 times. Fasten off, turn.
Round 5: Rep round 4 using yarn D. Fasten off, turn.
Round 6: Join yarn E in any corner 2ch-sp *(4 ch (counts as 1 htr, 2ch), 1 htr, 1 ch) in corner space, (1 htr, 1 ch) in each ch-sp to corner space, *(1 htr, 2 ch, 1 htr, 1 ch) in corner space, (1 htr, 1 ch) in each ch-sp to corner space; rep from * 4 times, sl st to join. Fasten off, do not turn.
Round 7: Join yarn F in any corner space, 6 ch (counts as 1 tr 2 ch), 1 tr in same corner space, 1 tr in top of each htr and in each ch-sp to corner, *(1 tr, 2 ch, 1 tr) in corner space, 1 tr in top of each htr and in each ch-sp to corner; rep from * 4 times, sl st to join. Fasten off.

Motif 63:
Nordic Hexagon

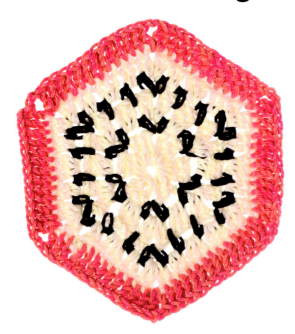

Double crochet stitches in black alternate with rounds of trebles to give this patterned effect.

Yarn A
130 Old Lace

Yarn C
114 Shocking Pink

Yarn B
110 Jet Black

Using yarn A, 6 ch, sl st to first ch to form a ring.
Round 1: 3 ch (counts as 1 tr), (2 tr, 2 ch) in ring, (3 tr, 2 ch) 5 times in ring, sl st in 3rd ch to join. Fasten off, turn.
Round 2: Join yarn B in any 2ch-sp, *(1 dc, 2 ch, 1 dc) in 2ch-sp, 3 ch; rep from * 5 times, sl st to join. Fasten off, turn.
Round 3: Join yarn A in corner 2ch-sp, 3 ch (counts as 1 tr), (1 tr, 2 ch, 2 tr) in 2ch-sp, 3 tr in 3ch-sp, *(2 tr, 2 ch, 2 tr) in 2ch-sp, 3 tr in 3ch-sp; rep from * 4 times, sl st to join. Fasten off, turn.
Round 4: Join yarn B in any corner 2ch-sp, *(1 dc, 2 ch, 1 dc) in 2ch-sp, 2 ch, 1 dc between trs, 3 ch, 1 dc between trs, 2 ch; rep from * 5 times, sl st to join. Fasten off, turn.
Round 5: Join yarn A in any corner 2ch-sp, (3 ch, 1 tr, 2 ch, 2 tr) in corner 2ch-sp, 2 tr in 2ch-sp, 3 tr in 3ch-sp, 2 tr in 2ch-sp, *(2 tr, 2 ch, 2 tr) in corner 2ch-sp, 2 tr in 2ch-sp, 3 tr in 3ch-sp, 2 tr in 2ch-sp; rep from * 4 times, sl st to join Fasten off, don't turn.
Round 6: Join yarn C in any corner 2ch-sp, [5 ch (counts as 1 tr, 2 ch), 1 tr] in same 2ch-sp, 1 tr in each tr to corner, *(1 tr, 2 ch, 1 tr) in corner 2ch-sp, 1 tr in each tr to corner; rep from * 4 times, sl st to join. Fasten off.

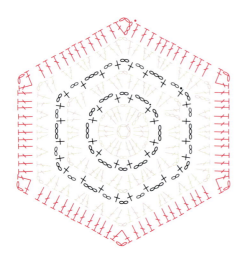

Motif 64:
Bobble Flower Hexagon

Working behind the bobble petals of this gorgeous little flower gives them even more impact.

Yarn A
249 Saffron

Yarn B
114 Shocking Pink

Yarn C
392 Lime Juice

Yarn D
400 Petrol Blue

Do not turn work throughout.
Using yarn A, 4 ch, sl st to first st to form a ring.
Round 1: Using yarn A, 2 ch (counts as 1 htr), 11 htr into ring, sl st to top of 2ch. Fasten off.
Round 2: Join yarn B in any htr, *2 ch in st, 1 bobble in next st, 3 ch, sl st into next st; rep from * 6 times, sl st in first st to join. Fasten off.
Round 3: Working in between petals join yarn C in htr between petal from round 1 with a sl st, 3 ch (counts as 1 tr), (2 tr, 2 ch, 3 tr) in same space, then move bobble up out way and work in next htr from round 1, *(3 tr, 2 ch, 3 tr) in same space, then move bobble up out way and work in next htr from round 1; rep from * 4 times, sl st into first 3 ch to join. Fasten off.
Round 4: Join yarn D in any corner space, 5 ch (counts as 1 tr, 2 ch), 1 tr in same corner, 1 tr in each tr to corner, *(1 tr, 2 ch, 1 tr) in corner space, 1 tr in each tr to corner; rep from * 4 times, sl st to join. Fasten off.

Notes
For instructions on bobble stitch, see page 20.

100 Essential Crochet Motifs

Motif 65:
Ribbed Hexagon

This hexagon gets its intricate design from front and back post trebles worked around the stitch posts.

Yarn A
249 Saffron

Do not turn work throughout.
Using yarn A, 6 ch, sl st to form a ring.
Round 1: 5 ch (counts as 1 tr, 2 ch), *(3 tr, 2 ch); rep from * 5 times, 2 tr, sl st into 3rd ch of beg 5 ch.
Round 2: Sl st into 2ch-sp, 5 ch, 1 tr in same 2ch-sp, 1 fptr round next st, 1 bptr round next tr, 1 fptr round next tr, *(1 tr, 2 ch, 1 tr) in 2ch-sp, 1 fptr round next st, 1 bptr round next tr, 1 fptr round next tr; rep from * 4 times, sl st into 3rd ch of 5 ch.
Round 3: Sl st into 2 ch corner space, 5 ch, 1 tr in same 2ch-sp, 1 bptr round next st, 1 fptr round next st, 1 bptr round next tr, 1 fptr round next tr, 1 bptr round next tr, *(1 tr, 2 ch, 1 tr) in 2ch-sp, 1 bptr round next st, 1 fptr round next st, 1 bptr round next tr, 1 fptr round next tr, 1 bptr round next tr; rep from * 4 times, sl st into 3rd ch of 5 ch.
Round 4: Sl st into 2 ch corner space, 5 ch, 1 tr in same 2ch-sp, 1 fptr round next st, 1 bptr round next st, 1 fptr round next st, 1 bptr round next tr, 1 fptr round next tr, 1 bptr round next tr, 1 fptr round next st, *(1 tr, 2 ch, 1 tr) in 2ch-sp, 1 fptr round next st, 1 bptr round next st, 1 fptr round next st, 1 bptr round next tr, 1 fptr round next tr, 1 bptr round next tr, 1 fptr round next st; rep from * 4 times, sl st into 3rd ch of 5 ch.
Round 5: Sl st into 2 ch corner space, 5 ch, 1 tr in same 2ch-sp, 1 bptr round next st, 1 fptr round next st, 1 bptr round next st, 1 fptr round next st, 1 bptr round next tr, 1 fptr round next tr, 1 bptr round next tr, 1 fptr round next st, 1 bptr round next st, *(1 tr, 2 ch, 1 tr) in 2ch-sp, 1 bptr round next st, 1 fptr round next st, 1 bptr round next st, 1 fptr round next st, 1 bptr round next tr, 1 fptr round next tr, 1 bptr round next tr, 1 fptr round next st, 1 bptr round next st; rep from * 4 times, sl st into 3rd ch of 5 ch. Fasten off.

Notes
For instructions on front post treble crochet (fptr) and back post treble crochet (bptr), see pages 18 and 19.

Motif 66:
Seventies Hexagon Flower

The colours and design of this groovy hexagon remind me of 1970s' style.

Yarn A ■
157 Root Beer

Yarn B ■
208 Yellow Gold

Yarn C ■
189 Royal Orange

Using yarn A, 6 ch, sl st to first st to form a ring.
Round 1: 3 ch (counts as 1 tr), 17 tr into ring, sl st to join. Fasten off, turn.
Round 2: Join yarn B in any tr with a *dc, 3 ch, miss 2 tr; rep from * 5 times, turn.
Round 3: Sl st into 3ch-sp, *(1 dc, 1 htr, 3 tr, 1 htr, 1 dc, 1 ch) in 3ch-sp; rep from * around, sl st into first dc to join. Fasten off, don't turn.
Round 4: Join yarn C in any ch-sp. 6 ch (counts as 1 dtr, 2 ch), 1 dtr in same space, 2 ch, 1 dc in 2nd of tr sts made in petal, 2 ch, *(1 dtr, 2 ch, 1 dtr) in ch-sp, 2 ch, 1 dc in 2nd of tr sts made in petal, 2 ch; rep from * 4 times, sl st into 4th of original 6 ch, do not turn.
Round 5: Sl st into 2ch-sp, 3 ch, 2 tr in same 2ch-sp, 3 tr in next 2ch-sp, (2 tr, 2 ch, 2 tr) in corner space, *3 tr in each of the next two 2ch-sps, (2 tr, 2 ch, 2 tr) in corner space; rep from * 4 times, sl st to join. Fasten off.

Motif 67:
Star Hexagon

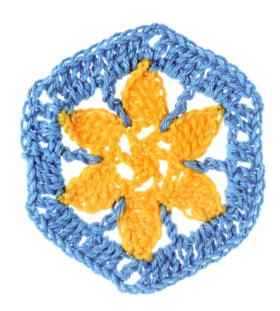

The star points in this lovely hexagon are made by working along chain stitches.

Yarn A
384 Powder Blue

Yarn B
208 Yellow Gold

Do not turn work throughout.
Using yarn A, 6 ch, sl st to first st to form a ring.
Round 1: 6 ch (counts as 1 tr, 3 ch), *(1 tr, 3 ch); rep from * 4 times, sl st to join.
Round 2: Sl st into top of tr, *6 ch (1 dc in 2nd ch, 1 htr in 3rd ch, 1 tr in next 3 ch), 1 dc in top of tr; rep from * 5 times. Fasten off.
Round 3: Join yarn B in any dc between star points, 7 ch (counts as 1 dtr, 3 ch), 1 dc in first dc at point of star, 3 ch, *(1 dtr, 3 ch) in dc between star points, 1 dc in first dc at point of star, 3 ch; rep from * 4 times, sl st to join.
Round 4: 3 ch (counts as 1 tr in the dtr), 3 tr in 3ch-sp, (1 tr, 2 ch, 1 tr) in dc at top of star point, 3 tr in next 3ch-sp, *1 tr in dtr, 3 tr in 3ch-sp, (1 tr, 2 ch, 1 tr) in dc at top of star point, 3 tr in next 3ch-sp; rep from * 4 times, sl st to join. Fasten off.

Motif 68:
Snowflake Hexagon

This lace-like hexagon would look gorgeous sewn into a baby's blanket or as a window decoration.

Yarn A
173 Bluebell

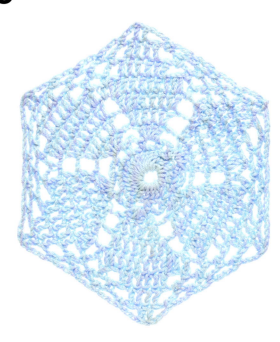

Do not turn work throughout.
With yarn A, ch 6, sl st to form a ring.
Round 1: 3 ch (counts as 1 tr), 23 tr in ring, sl st in top of 3 ch.
Round 2: (3 ch, miss 1 tr, 1 dc in next st) 12 times around, sl st in starting 3ch-sp.
Round 3: (3 ch, 3 tr) in same 3ch-sp, 2 ch, skip next 3ch-sp, *4 tr in next 3ch-sp, 2 ch, skip next 3ch-sp; rep from * 4 times, sl st in top of 3 ch.
Round 4: (3 ch, 1 tr) in same tr, 2 tr, 2 tr in next tr, 2 ch, *(2 tr in next tr, 2 tr, 2 tr in next tr), 2 ch; rep from * 4 times, sl st in top of 3 ch.
Round 5: (3 ch, 1 tr) in same tr, 4 tr, 2 tr in next tr, 2 ch, *(2 tr in next tr, 4 tr, 2 tr in next tr), 2 ch; rep from * 4 times, sl st in top of 3 ch.
Round 6: (3 ch, 1 tr) in same tr, 6 tr, 2 tr in next tr, (3 ch, 1 dc, 3 ch) in 2ch-sp, *2 tr in next tr, 6 tr, 2 tr in next tr, (3 ch, 1 dc, 3 ch) in 2ch-sp; rep from * 4 times, sl st in top of 3 ch.
Round 7: Sl st to 3rd tr of 10 tr group, 3 ch, 5 tr, 3 ch, 1 dc in next 3ch-sp, 3 ch, 1 dc in next 3ch-sp, 3 ch, miss 2 tr, *6 tr, (3 ch, 1 dc in next 3ch-sp) twice, 3 ch; rep from * 4 times, sl st in top of 3 ch.
Round 8: Sl st to 2nd tr of 6 tr group, 3 ch, 3 tr, (3 ch, 1 dc in next 3ch-sp) 3 times, 3 ch, miss 1 tr, *4 tr, (3 ch, 1 dc in next 3ch-sp) 3 times, 3 ch; rep from * 4 times, sl st in top of 3 ch.
Round 9: Sl st across next tr, sl st in space before next tr, 3 ch, 1 tr in same sp, (3 ch, 1 dc in next 3ch-sp) 4 times, 3 ch, *miss 2 tr, 2 tr in space before next tr, (3 ch, 1 dc in next 3ch-sp) 4 times, 3 ch; rep from * 4 times, sl st in top of 3 ch. Fasten off.

Motif 69:
Scandi Hexagon

The colours and shapes of this hexagon remind me of gorgeous Scandinavian knitwear.

Yarn A
242 Metal Grey

Yarn B
130 Old Lace

Do not turn work throughout.
Using yarn A, 4 ch, sl st to first st to form a ring.
Round 1: Using yarn A, 6 dc in 4 ch ring, sl st to join.
Round 2: 1 ch (doesn't count as a st), 2 dc in each dc around.
Round 3: 1 ch (doesn't count as a st), *1 dc, in next dc, (1 tr, 1 ch, 1 tr) in next dc; rep from * 5 times, sl st to join. Fasten off.
Round 4: Join yarn B in any ch-sp, *1 dc in ch-sp, (2 tr, 1 ch, 2 tr) in dc; rep from * 5 times, sl st into first dc to join. Fasten off.
Round 5: Join yarn A in any ch-sp, *1 dc in ch-sp, (3 tr, 1 ch, 3 tr) in dc; rep from * 5 times, sl st into first dc to join. Fasten off.
Round 6: Join yarn B in any ch-sp, *1 dc in ch-sp, (4 tr, 1 ch, 4 tr) in dc; rep from * 5 times, sl st into first dc to join. Fasten off.

Motif 70:
Openwork Circle

You could adapt this chain stitch edging for other crochet projects to give a lovely finish.

Yarn A
384 Powder Blue

Yarn C
258 Rosewood

Yarn B
253 Tropic

Yarn D
130 Old Lace

Turn after each round.
Using yarn A, 6 ch, sl st to first st to form a ring.
Round 1: 3 ch (counts as 1 tr), 17 tr into ring, sl st to join, turn. Fasten off.
Round 2: Join yarn B in any tr, 4 ch (counts as 1 tr, 1 ch), 1 tr and 1 ch in each tr around, sl st to 3 ch to join. Fasten off.
Round 3: Join yarn C in any ch-sp, 3 ch (counts as first tr of tr3tog), tr2tog, (2 ch, tr3tog) in each sp around, 2 ch, sl st to join. Fasten off.
Round 4: Join yarn D in any 2ch-sp, *1 dc, 3 ch, (1 tr, 3 ch, 1 tr, 3 ch) in next 2ch-sp, (1 dc, 3 ch) in next 2ch-sp; rep from * 5 times, sl st to join.

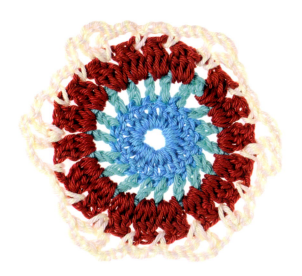

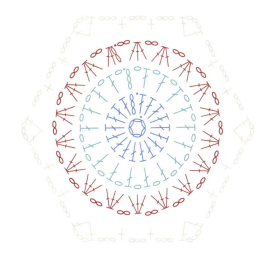

Motif 71:
Solid Triangle

This colourful triangle is simple to scale up to any size you like – just keep on repeating round 2!

Yarn A
411 Sweet Orange

Yarn C
114 Shocking Pink

Yarn B
409 Soft Rose

Yarn D
130 Old Lace

Do not turn work throughout.
Using yarn A, 6 ch, sl st to first st to form a ring.
Round 1: 3 ch (counts as 1 tr), 3 tr into ring, 5 ch, (4 tr, 5 ch) twice, sl st to join. Fasten off.
Round 2: Join yarn B in any corner 5ch-sp, 3 ch (counts as 1 tr), (2 tr, 5 ch, 3 tr) in same space, 1 tr in each tr to corner 5ch-sp, *(3 tr, 5 ch, 3 tr) in 5ch-sp, 1 tr in each tr to corner 5ch-sp; rep from * once more, sl st to join. Fasten off.
Round 3: Rep round 2 using yarn C.
Round 4: Rep round 2 using yarn D.

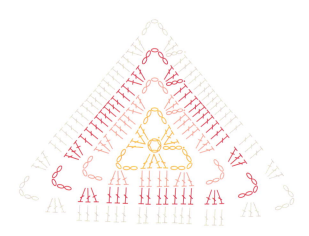

96   100 Essential Crochet Motifs

Motif 72:
Granny Triangle

Just like the traditional granny square, this triangle uses groups of trebles and chains.

Yarn A
164 Light Navy

Yarn B
384 Powder Blue

Yarn C
513 Apple Granny

Yarn D
130 Old Lace

Do not turn work throughout.
Using yarn A, 6 ch, sl st to first st to form a ring.
Round 1: 3 ch (counts as 1 tr), 3 tr into ring, 5 ch, (4 tr, 5 ch) twice, sl st to join. Fasten off.
Round 2: Using yarn B, join yarn in any corner 5ch-sp, 3 ch (counts as 1 tr), (3 tr, 5 ch, 4 tr) in same space, *(4 tr, 5 ch, 4 tr) in next space; rep from * once more, sl st to join. Fasten off.
Round 3: Using yarn C, join yarn in any corner 5ch-sp, 3 ch (counts as 1 tr), (3 tr, 5 ch, 4 tr) in same space, 4 tr in each sp to corner, *(4 tr, 5 ch, 4 tr) in corner space, 4 tr in each sp to corner; rep from * once more, sl st to join. Fasten off.
Round 4: Rep round 3 using yarn D.

Motif 73:
African Violet-style Triangle

Here spike double crochet stitches create the outline for these vibrant pink petals.

Yarn A
252 Watermelon

Yarn B
409 Soft Rose

Yarn C
164 Light Navy

Using yarn A, 6 ch, sl st to first st to form a ring, do not turn.

Round 1: 3 ch (counts as 1 tr), (1 tr, 1 ch, 2 tr, 2 ch) into ring, (2 tr, 1 ch, 2 tr, 2 ch) twice more, sl st to join, turn.

Round 2: Sl st into corner 2ch-sp, 3 ch (counts as 1 tr), 8 tr into 2ch-sp, 9 tr into next 2ch-sp twice more, sl st to join. Fasten off, turn.

Round 3: Join yarn B into the first of any 9 tr, *1 dc in each of 9 tr, 1 Sp-dc in ch-sp from round 1; rep from * twice more, sl st to join, do not turn.

Round 4: Join yarn C in the 5th dc of set of 9 dc, 4 ch (counts as 1 dtr), (1 dtr, 3 ch, 2 dtr) in same st, 1 tr in next st, 1 htr in next 7 sts, 1 tr in next st, *(2 dtr, 3 ch, 2 dtr) in next st, 1 tr in next st, 1 htr in next 7 sts, 1 tr in next st; rep from * once more, sl st to join.

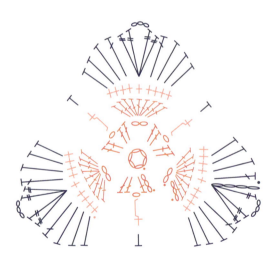

Notes
For instructions on spike double crochet stitches (Sp-dc), see page 19.

Motif 74:
Ribbed Triangle

This vibrant green triangle uses front and back post treble stitches to create the ribbing.

Yarn A
389 Apple Green

Do not turn work throughout.
Using yarn A, 4 ch, sl st to first st to form a ring.
Round 1: 5 ch (counts as 1 tr, 2 ch), (3 tr, 2 ch) into ring twice, 2 tr, sl st to join.
Round 2: Sl st into 2 ch corner space, 3 ch, (1 tr, 2 ch, 2 tr) in same 2ch-sp, work fptr round next st, bptr round next tr, frptc round next tr, *(2 tr, 2 ch, 2 tr) in 2ch-sp, fptr round next st, bptr round next tr, frptc round next tr; rep from * once more, sl st into top of 3 ch to join.
Round 3: Sl st into 2 ch corner space, 3 ch (1 tr, 2 ch, 2 tr) tr in same 2ch-sp, work *fptr round next st, bptr round next st; rep from * along to corner ending with a fptr round last tr, **(2 tr, 2 ch, 2 tr) in 2ch-sp, *fptr round next st, bptr round next st; rep from * along to corner ending with a fptr around last tr; rep from ** once more, sl st into top of 3 ch to join.
Round 4: Rep round 3.
Round 5: Rep round 3.

Notes
For instructions on front post treble crochet (fptr) and back post treble crochet (bptr), see pages 18 and 19.

100 Essential Crochet Motifs

Motif 75:
Circle in a Triangle

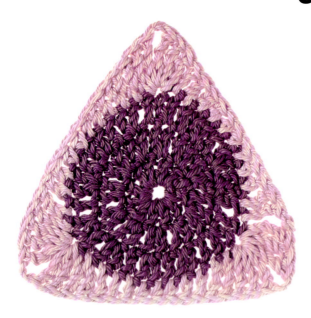

You can use the technique here to convert a larger circle to a triangle using variations of treble stitches.

Yarn A
113 Delphinium

Yarn B
226 Light Orchid

Do not turn work throughout.
Using yarn A, 4 ch, sl st to form a ring.

Round 1: 3 ch (counts as 1 tr), 11 tr in ring, sl st to join.

Round 2: (3 ch, 1 tr) in same tr, 2 tr in each tr around, sl st to join.

Round 3: (3 ch, 1 tr) in same tr, 1 tr, (2 tr in next tr, 1 tr) around, sl st to join. Fasten off.

Round 4: Join yarn B in any st, 5 ch (counts as 1 trtr), (2 trtr, 2 ch, 3 trtr) in same st, 1 dtr in next 2 sts, 1 tr in next 2 sts, 1 htr in next 3 sts, 1 tr in next 2 sts, 1 dtr in next 2 sts, *(3 trtr, 2 ch, 3 trtr) in next st, 1 dtr in next 2 sts, 1 tr in next 2 sts, 1 htr in next 3 sts, 1 tr in next 2 sts, 1 dtr in next 2 sts; rep from * once more, sl st to join. Fasten off.

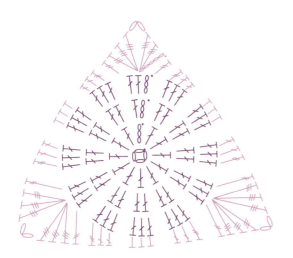

Notes
For instructions on triple treble (trtr), see page 15.

Motif 76:
Hexagon to Triangle

This motif uses double crochet edging and longer treble variations to create the points of the triangle.

Yarn A
189 Royal Orange

Yarn C
411 Sweet Orange

Yarn B
222 Tulip

Yarn D
130 Old Lace

Turn after each round.
Using yarn A, 4 ch, sl st to first st to form a ring.
Round 1: 3 ch (counts as 1 tr), (1 tr, 2 ch into ring), *(2 tr, 2 ch) into ring; repeat from * 4 times, sl st to top of 3 ch to join. Fasten off.
Round 2: Join yarn B in any 2ch-sp, 3 ch (counts as 1 tr), (1 tr, 2 ch, 2 tr) in same 2ch-sp, (2 tr, 2 ch, 2 tr) in each 2ch-sp around, sl st to join. Fasten off.
Round 3: Join yarn C in any 2ch-sp, 3 ch, (1 tr, 2 ch, 2 tr) in same 2ch-sp, 2 tr in space between sets of 2 tr, *(2 tr, 2 ch, 2 tr) in same 2ch-sp, 2 tr in space between sets of 2 tr; rep from * 4 times, sl st to join. Fasten off.
Round 4: Join yarn D in any 2ch-sp, *1 dc, 1 htr in next st, 1 tr in next st, 2 dtr in next st, 2 ch, 2 dtr in next st, 1 tr, 1 htr 1 dc, 1 dc in each tr to next corner space; rep from * twice more, sl st to join. Fasten off.

100 Essential Crochet Motifs

Motif 77:
Flower in Mesh Triangle

I love the contrast between the bright flower and the delicate chain-stitch mesh in this motif.

Yarn A 🟨
208 Yellow Gold

Yarn B 🟦
173 Bluebell

Yarn B 🟦
146 Vivid Blue

Turn after each round.
Using yarn A, 4 ch, sl st to first st to form a ring.

Round 1: 1 ch (doesn't count as a stitch), 9 htr into ring, sl st into first htr. Fasten off.

Round 2: Join yarn B in any htr, 3 ch (counts as first part of dtr3tog), dtr2tog in same sp, 3 ch, (dtr3tog, 3 ch) in each tr around sl st to join. Fasten off.

Round 3: Join yarn C in any 3ch-sp with a dc, 4 ch, 1 dc in next 3ch-sp, (5 ch, 1 dc, 7 ch, 1 dc) in next 3ch-sp, *5 ch, 1 dc in next 3ch-sp, 4 ch, 1 dc in next 3ch-sp, (5 ch, 1 dc, 7 ch, 1 dc) in same 3ch-sp; rep from * once more, 5 ch, sl st into beg dc.

Round 4: Sl st into next 4ch-sp, 1 ch, 1 dc in same space, (5 ch, 1 dc) in next ch-sp, twice, 7 ch and 1 dc in same space, *(5 ch, 1 dc in next sp) 4 times, 7 ch and 1 dc in same space; rep from * once more, 5 ch, dc in next ch-sp, 5 ch, sl st into beg dc. Fasten off.

Motif 78:
Cartwheel Triangle

This design reminds me of a spinning firework, or a child with bright red boots doing a cartwheel!

Yarn A
114 Shocking Pink

Yarn C
390 Poppy Rose

Yarn B
264 Light Coral

Yarn D
130 Old Lace

Turn after each round.
Using yarn A, 6 ch, sl st to first st to form a ring.
Round 1: 3 ch (counts as 1 tr), 11 tr into ring, sl st into first tr. Fasten off, turn.
Round 2: Join yarn B in any tr, 4 ch (counts as 1 tr, 1 ch), 1 tr, 1 ch in each tr around, sl st to join. Fasten off, turn.
Round 3: Join yarn C in any ch-sp, 2 ch (counts as first part of tr3tog), tr2tog in same space, 3 ch, (tr3tog, 3 ch) in each ch-sp around, sl st to join. Fasten off, turn.
Round 4: Join yarn D in any 3ch-sp, 3 ch (counts as 1 tr), (4 tr, 3 ch, 5 tr) in same 3ch-sp, (3 ch 1 dc in next 3ch-sp) 3 times, 3 ch, *(5 tr, 3 ch, 5 tr) in next 3ch-sp, (3 ch, 1 dc in next 3ch-sp) 3 times, 3 ch; rep from * once more, sl st to join. Fasten off.

100 Essential Crochet Motifs

Motif 79:
In a Whirl Triangle

I used double trebles to create the long spokes at the centre of this pretty triangle.

Yarn A 🟨
280 Lemon

Yarn C
130 Old Lace

Yarn B 🟥
251 Garden Rose

Turn after each round.
Using yarn A, 4 ch, sl st to first st to form a ring.
Round 1: 6 ch (counts as 1 dtr, 2 ch), (1 dtr, 2 ch) 11 times into ring, sl st into 4th ch of 6 ch to join. Fasten off, turn.
Round 2: Join yarn B in any 2ch-sp, 4 ch (counts as 1 dtr), (2 dtr, 2 ch, 3 dtr) in same 2ch-sp, 2 dtr in each of the next 3 3ch-sps, *(3 dtr, 2 ch, 3 dtr) in next 2ch-sp, 2 dtr in each of the next 3 3ch-sps; rep from * once more, sl st to join. Fasten off, turn.
Round 3: Join yarn C in any corner 2ch-sp, 3 ch (counts as 1 tr), (1 tr, 2 ch, 2 tr) in corner space, 1 tr in each tr to corner space, *(2 tr, 2 ch, 2 tr) in corner space, 1 tr in each tr to corner space; rep from * once more, sl st to join. Fasten off.

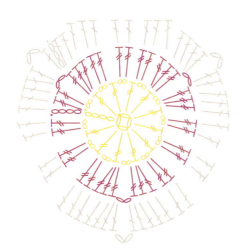

104   100 Essential Crochet Motifs

Motif 80:
Triangle Flower

I've chosen vibrant shades and puff stitches to give this gorgeous flower extra impact.

Yarn A
189 Royal Orange

Yarn C
205 Kiwi

Yarn B
222 Tulip

Do not turn work throughout.
Using yarn A, 6 ch, sl st to first st to form a ring.
Round 1: (1 BegPuff, 3 ch), (1 puff, 3 ch) 8 times, sl st into top of BegPuff to join.
Round 2: Join yarn B in any 3ch-sp (1 BegPuff, 1 ch, 1 puff, 6 ch) in same 3ch-sp, * (1 puff, 1 ch, 1 puff, 1 ch) in next 3ch-sp, (1 puff, 1 ch, 1 puff, 1 ch) in next 3ch-sp, (1 puff, 1 ch, 1 puff, 6 ch) in next 3ch-sp; rep from * once; (1 puff, 1 ch, 1 puff, 1 ch) in next 3ch-sp, (1 puff, 1 ch, 1 puff, 1 ch) in next 3ch-sp, sl st to join.
Round 3: Join yarn C in any 6ch-sp (1 BegPuff, 1 ch, 1 puff, 7 ch, 1 puff, 1 ch, 1 puff, 1 ch), in same 6ch-sp, miss 1 puff, (1 puff, 1 ch, 1 puff, 1 ch) in next ch-sp, miss 1 puff, (1 puff, 1 ch, 1 puff, 1 ch) in next ch-sp, miss 1 puff, (1 puff, 1 ch, 1 puff, 1 ch) in next ch-sp, *(1 puff, 1 ch, 1 puff, 7 ch, 1 puff, 1 ch, 1 puff, 1 ch) in 6ch-sp, miss 1 puff, (1 puff, 1 ch, 1 puff, 1 ch) in next ch-sp, miss 1 puff, (1 puff, 1 ch, 1 puff, 1 ch) in next ch-sp, miss 1 puff, (1 puff, 1 ch, 1 puff, 1 ch) in next ch-sp; rep from * once more, sl st to join. Fasten off.

Notes
This design uses puff and beginning puff (BegPuff) stitches. For instructions, see page 17.

100 Essential Crochet Motifs

Motif 81:
Openwork Triangle

I really love this design, which combines openwork chain stitches with dense sets of trebles.

Yarn A
114 Shocking Pink

Yarn B
113 Delphinium

Yarn C
226 Light Orchid

Do not turn work throughout.
Using yarn A, 6 ch, sl st to first st to form a ring.
Round 1: 3 ch (counts as 1 tr), 14 tr into ring, sl st to join. Fasten off.
Round 2: Join yarn B in any tr, 3 ch (counts as 1 tr), 6 tr in same tr, 4 ch, miss 4 tr), *7 tr in next tr, 4 ch, miss 4 tr; rep from * once more, sl st into top of 3 ch to join. Fasten off.
Round 3: Join yarn C in the first tr of any of the sets of 7 tr, 3 ch (counts as first tr), 1 tr in next 2 tr, miss 1 tr, 7 ch, 1 tr in next 3 tr, 4 ch, miss, 4 ch, *1 tr next 3 tr, miss 1 tr, 7 ch, 1 tr in next 3 tr, 4 ch, miss, 4 ch; rep from * once more, sl st into top of first 3 ch.
Round 4: 3 ch (counts as first tr), 1 tr in next 2 tr, (6 tr, 3 ch, 6 tr) in next 7ch-sp, 1 tr in next 3 tr, 5 ch, miss 4 ch, *1 tr in next 3 tr, (6 tr, 3 ch, 6 tr) in next 7ch-sp, 1 tr in next 3 tr, 5 ch, miss 4 ch; rep from * once more, sl st to join. Fasten off.

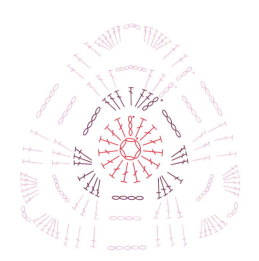

100 Essential Crochet Motifs

Motif 82:
Ivy's Triangle

The contrasting, bright puff stitches at the centre give real impact to this triangle design.

Yarn A
146 Vivid Blue

Yarn C
114 Shocking Pink

Yarn B
189 Royal Orange

Do not turn work throughout.
Using yarn A, 6 ch, sl st to first st to form a ring.
Round 1: 1 BegPuff, 3 ch, (1 puff, 3 ch) 5 times, sl st into top of BegPuff to join. Fasten off.
Round 2: Join Yarn B in any 3ch-sp, 1 ch (doesn't count as a st), 1 dc, 8 ch, miss 1 puff, 1 dc in next 3 ch, 4 ch, *1 dc in next 3ch-sp, 8 ch, miss 1 puff, 1 dc in next 3 ch, 4 ch; rep from * once more, sl st into first dc.
Round 3: Sl st into 4ch-sp, 1 ch (doesn't count as a st), *1 dc in 4ch-sp, (5 tr, 3 ch, 5 tr) in 8 ch-sp; rep from * twice more, sl st to join.
Round 4: Join yarn C in any 3ch-sp, 1 ch (doesn't count as a st), *1 dc in 3 ch corner space, 4 ch, 1 dc in same space, 3 ch, miss 2 tr, 1 dc in 3rd of 5 tr below, 3 ch, 1 dc in dc, 3 ch, 1 dc in 3rd of 5 tr, 3 ch; rep from * twice more, sl st into first dc.
Round 5: Sl st into corner 4ch-sp, 3 ch (counts as 1 tr), (2 tr, 1 ch, 1 dtr, 1 ch, 3 tr) in corner 4ch-sp, 1 ch, 2 tr in each of the 3ch-sps to corner, 1 ch, *(3 tr, 1 ch, 1 dtr, 1 ch, 3 tr) in corner 4ch-sp, 1 ch, 2 tr in each of the 3ch-sps to corner, 1 ch; rep from * once more, sl st to join.

Notes
This design uses puff and beginning puff (BegPuff) stitches, see page 17.

Motif 83:
Moss Stitch Triangle

This motif looks more difficult than it is! Alternating rounds of colour create the moss-stitch effect.

Yarn A
201 Electric Blue

Yarn B
130 Old Lace

Do not turn work throughout.
Using yarn A, 6 ch, sl st to first st to form a ring.
Round 1: 3 ch (counts as 1 tr), 4 tr, 5 ch, (5 tr, 5 ch) twice, sl st into top of 3 ch to join. Fasten off.
Round 2: Join yarn B in any 5ch-sp, *(1 dc, 1 ch, 1 dc, 2 ch, 1 dc, 1 ch, 1 dc, 1 ch) in 5ch-sp, (1 dc, 1 ch) in each sp between trs to corner space; rep from * twice more. Fasten off.
Round 3: Join yarn A in any 2ch-sp, *(1 dc, 2 ch, 1 dc, 1 ch) in 2ch-sp, work (1 dc, 1 ch) in each sp between dcs to corner space; rep from * twice more, sl st to join. Fasten off.
Round 4: Rep round 3 using yarn B.
Round 5: Rep round 3 using yarn A.
Round 6: Rep round 3 using yarn B.
Round 7: Rep round 3 using yarn A.

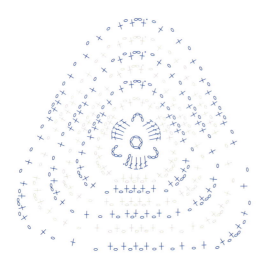

Notes
For the alternating rounds of yarn A and yarn B, fasten off the yarn at the end of each round, then sew in the ends through stitches of the same yarn colour.

Motif 84:
Perfect Petal Triangle

This gorgeous petal design is created with double treble and treble together stitches.

Yarn A
255 Shell

Yarn C
130 Old Lace

Yarn B
264 Light Coral

Do not turn work throughout.
Using yarn A, 6 ch, sl st to first st to form a ring.
Round 1: 3 ch (counts as 1 tr in tr3tog), tr2tog, 5 ch, tr3tog, 3 ch, *tr3tog, 5 ch, tr3tog, 3 ch; rep from * once more, sl st into top of 3 ch to join.
Round 2: Sl st into first 5ch-sp, (3 ch, tr2tog, 4 ch, dtr3tog, 4 ch, tr3tog) in 5ch-sp, 3 ch, 1 ch in 3ch-sp, 3 ch, *(tr3tog, 4 ch, dtr3tog, 4 ch, tr3tog) in 5ch-sp, 3 ch, 1 ch in 3ch-sp, 3 ch; rep from * once more, sl st to join. Fasten off.
Round 3: Join yarn B in the top of any dtr3tog, 3 ch (counts as 1 tr), (1 tr, 3 ch, 2 tr) in dtr3tog, 5 tr in next 4ch-sp, 4 tr in each of the next two 3ch-sps, 5 tr in next 4ch-sp, *(2 tr, 3 ch, 2 tr) in dtr2tog, 5 tr in next 4ch-sp, 4 tr in each of the next two 3ch-sps, 5 tr in next 4ch-sp; rep from * once more, sl st to join. Fasten off.
Round 4: Join yarn C in any 3ch-sp, 3 ch (counts as 1 tr), (1 tr, 3 ch, 2 tr) in corner space, 1 tr in each tr to corner space, *(2 tr, 3 ch, 2 tr) in corner space, 1 tr in each tr to corner space; rep from * once more, sl st to join. Fasten off.

Notes
This motif uses treble 3 together stitches (tr3tog). See pages 14 and 15 for instructions.

Double treble 3 together (dtr3tog) are worked in exactly the same way as treble 3 together, using double trebles (see page 13) instead of trebles.

100 Essential Crochet Motifs

Motif 85:
Heart Triangle

String several of these hearts together to make a lovely garland for a special person.

Yarn A
252 Watermelon

Yarn B
130 Old Lace

Yarn C
256 Cornelia Rose

Do not turn work throughout.
Using yarn A, 4 ch, sl st to first st to form a ring.
Round 1: 3 ch, 3 dtr, 3 tr, 1 ch, 1 dtr, 1 ch, 3 tr, 3 dtr, into ring, 3 ch, sl st into ring. Fasten off.
Round 2: Join yarn B in between 3 ch and first st in ring, 4 ch (counts as 1 dtr), 1 dtr in first ch, 1 tr in next 2 chs, 1 htr in next st, 2 dc in each of next 2 sts, 1 htr in next 2 sts, 1 tr in next 2 sts, 3 dc, 1 tr in next 2 sts, 1 htr in next 2 sts, 2 dc in each of next 2 sts, 1 htr in next st, 1 tr in next 2 chs, 1 dtr in last ch, sl st to join.
Round 3: 2 ch counts as 1 htr, 1 htr in same st, 1 htr in next st, *2 htr, in next st, 1 htr in next st; rep from * around, sl st into first 3 ch to join. Fasten off.
Round 4: Join yarn C in top of last st from previous round, 4 ch, (1 dtr, 3 ch, 2 dtr) in same stitch, 1 dtr in next st, 1 tr in next 2 sts, 1 htr in next 2 sts, 1 dc in next 3 sts, 1 htr in next 2 sts, 1 tr in next 2 sts, 1 dtr in next st, *(2 dtr, 3 ch, 2 dtr) in same stitch, 1 dtr in next st, 1 tr in next 2 sts, 1 htr in next 2 sts, 1 dc in next 3 sts, 1 htr in next 2 sts, 1 tr in next 2 sts, 1 dtr in next st; rep from * once more. Fasten off.

Motif 86:
Solid Octagon

This is another motif that can be made as big as you like! Just keep repeating round 3 in different yarn.

Yarn A
114 Shocking Pink

Yarn B
519 Freesia

Yarn C
389 Apple Green

Yarn D
241 Parrot Green

Yarn E
130 Old Lace

Do not turn work throughout.
Using yarn A, 4 ch, sl st to first st to form a ring.
Round 1: 4 ch (counts as 1 tr, 1 ch), (1 tr, 1 ch) 7 times into ring, sl st into 3rd ch to join. Fasten off, turn.
Round 2: Using yarn B, join yarn in any ch-sp, 4 ch, 1 tr in same ch-sp, 1 tr in top of next tr, *(1 tr, 1 ch, 1 tr) in next ch-sp, 1 tr in tr; rep from * 6 times, sl st to join, turn. Fasten off.
Round 3: Using yarn C, join yarn in any ch-sp, 4 ch, 1 tr in same ch-sp, 1 tr in each tr to corner, *(1 tr, 1 ch, 1 tr) in next ch-sp, 1 tr in each tr to corner; rep from * 6 times, sl st to join, turn. Fasten off.
Round 4: Rep round 3 using yarn D.
Round 5: Rep round 3 using yarn E.

100 Essential Crochet Motifs

Motif 87:
Puff Stitch Octagon

The puff stitches at the centre of this octagon give a lovely texture to this motif.

Yarn A
208 Yellow Gold

Yarn B
189 Royal Orange

Yarn C
251 Garden Rose

Yarn D
130 Old Lace

Do not turn work throughout.
Using yarn A, 6 ch, sl st to first st to form a ring.
Round 1: (1 BegPuff, 2 ch), (1 puff, 2 ch) 7 times, sl st into top of BegPuff to join.
Round 2: Join Yarn B in any 2ch-sp, (1 BegPuff, 1 ch, 1 puff, 2 ch) in same 2ch-sp, (1 puff, 1 ch, 1 puff, 2 ch) in each 2ch-sp around, sl st to join.
Round 3: Join yarn C in any ch-sp, 3 ch (counts as 1 tr), (1 tr, 2 ch, 2 tr) in same ch-sp, 2 tr in 2ch-sp, *(2 tr, 2 ch, 2 tr) in next ch-sp, 2 tr in 2ch-sp; rep from * 6 times, sl st to join. Fasten off.
Round 4: Join Yarn D in any 2ch-sp, 4 ch (counts as 1 tr, 1 ch), 1 tr in same 2ch-sp, 1 tr in each tr to corner 2ch-sp, *(1 tr, 1 ch, 1 tr) in next 2ch-sp, 1 tr in each tr to corner 2ch-sp; rep from * 6 times, sl st to join. Fasten off.

> **Notes**
> This design uses beginning puff (BegPuff) and puff stitches. For instructions, see page 17.

Motif 88:
Sophia Octagon

I love the contrast here between the delicate design and the impact of its pink centre.

Yarn A
511 Cornflower Blue

Yarn B
114 Shocking Pink

Yarn C
280 Lemon

Yarn D
385 Crystalline

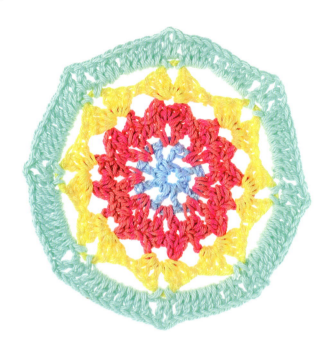

Turn after each round.
Using yarn A, 6 ch, sl st to first st to form a ring.
Round 1: 5 ch (counts as 1 tr, 2 ch), (1 tr, 2 ch) 7 times into ring, sl st to join. Fasten off.
Round 2: Join yarn B in any 2ch-sp, *(1 dc, 5 ch, 1 dc) in 2ch-sp, 3 ch, miss 1 tr; rep from * 7 times, sl st to first dc.
Round 3: Sl st into first 5ch-sp, 2 ch (counts as 1 htr), (1 htr, 4 ch, 2 htr) in 5ch-sp, 1 dc in 3ch-sp, *(2 htr, 4 ch, 2 htr) in 5ch-sp, 1 dc in 3ch-sp; rep from * 6 times, sl st to top of 2 ch to join. Fasten off.
Round 4: Join Yarn C in any 4ch-sp, 3 ch (counts as 1 tr), (2 tr, 2 ch, 3 tr) in 4ch-sp, *(3 tr, 2 ch, 3 tr) in each 4ch-sp around, sl st into top of 3 ch to join. Fasten off.
Round 5: Join Yarn D in top of any 2ch-sp *(1 dc, 3 ch, 1 dc) in 3ch-sp, 7 ch; rep from *7 times, sl st to join.
Round 6: Sl st into 3ch-sp, 4 ch (counts as 1 tr, 1 ch), 1 tr in same space, 8 tr in 7ch-sp, *(1 tr, 1 ch, 1 tr) in 3ch-sp space, 8 tr in 7ch-sp; rep from * 6 times, sl st to join. Fasten off.

Motif 89:
Openwork Octagon

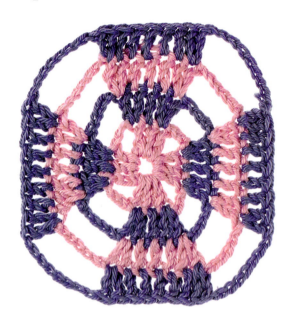

This design reminds me of a Celtic Cross, with chain stitches forming 4 sides of the octagon.

Yarn A
398 Colonial Rose

Yarn B
508 Deep Amethyst

Do not turn work throughout.
Using yarn A, 3 ch, sl st to first st to form a ring.
Round 1: 3 ch (counts as 1 tr), (2 tr, 3 ch), (3 tr, 3 ch) 3 times, sl st to join.
Round 2: Using yarn B, 3 ch (counts as 1 tr), 1 tr in the same tr, 1 tr in next tr, 2 tr in next tr, 5 ch, *2 tr in the next tr, 1 tr in next tr, 2 tr in next tr, 5 ch; rep from * twice more, sl st to join. Fasten off.
Round 3: Using yarn A, 3 ch (counts as 1 tr), 1 tr in the same tr, 1 tr in each tr to last tr, 2 tr in next tr, 7 ch, *2 tr in the next tr, 1 tr in each tr to last tr, 2 tr in next tr, 7 ch; rep from * twice more, sl st to join. Fasten off.
Round 4: Using yarn B, 3 ch (counts as 1 tr), 1 tr in the same tr, 1 tr in each tr to last tr, 2 tr in next tr, 9 ch, *2 tr in the next tr, 1 tr in each tr to last tr, 2 tr in next tr, 9 ch; rep from * twice more, sl st to join. Fasten off.

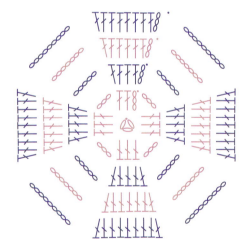

Motif 90:
African Violet Octagon

As with all my African Violet designs, I've used spike stitches and double crochet to edge the flowers here.

Yarn A 🟧
281 Tangerine

Yarn D 🟪
238 Powder Pink

Yarn B 🟦
201 Electric Blue

Yarn E 🟨
208 Yellow Gold

Yarn C 🟥
114 Shocking Pink

Do not turn work throughout.
Using yarn A, 5 ch, sl st to first st to form a ring.
Round 1: 3 ch (counts as 1 tr), (1 tr, 1 ch), (2 tr, 1 ch) 7 times, sl st to join.
Round 2: Join yarn B in any ch-sp, 3 ch (counts as 1 tr), (1 tr, 1 ch, 2 tr) in ch-sp, (2 tr, 1 ch, 2 tr) in each ch-sp around, sl st into top of first 3 ch to join.
Round 3: Sl st into ch-sp, 3 ch (counts as 1 tr), 6 tr in same ch-sp, 7 tr in each of the ch-sps around, sl st to join.
Round 4: Join yarn C in any of the first tr in groups of 7 tr, *1 dc in each of next 7 tr, 1 Sp-tr (see Notes) in space between 2 tr groups below in row 2; rep from * around, sl st to first dc to join.
Round 5: Join yarn D in the 4th dc of any of the groups of 7 dc, 4 ch, (counts as 1 tr, 1 ch), 1 tr in same st, 1 tr in the next 7 sts, *(1 tr, 1 ch, 1 tr) in the next tr, 1 tr in the next 7 sts; rep from * 6 times, sl st to join.
Round 6: Join yarn E in any ch-sp, *(1 dc, 1 ch, 1 dc) in corner space, miss first tr, 1 dc in each of next 7 tr, miss last dc; rep from * 7 times, sl st to join. Fasten off.

Notes
This motif uses spike treble stitches (Sp-tr). For instructions, see page 19.

Motif 91:
Blue Haze Octagon

I love the contrast between the bright red treble 4 togethers and the blue shades here.

Yarn A
201 Electric Blue

Yarn B
397 Cyan

Yarn C
252 Watermelon

Yarn D
146 Vivid Blue

Yarn E
173 Bluebell

Turn after each round.

Using yarn A, 6 ch, sl st to first st to form a ring.

Round 1: 3 ch (counts as 1 tr), 1 tr into ring 15 times, sl st to join. Fasten off.

Round 2: Join yarn B in any tr, 4 ch (counts as 1 tr, 1 ch), (1 tr, 1 ch) in each tr around, sl st into 3rd ch to join. Fasten off, turn.

Round 3: Join yarn C in any ch-sp, 3 ch (counts as first part of tr4tog), tr3tog in same space, 2 ch, (tr4tog, 2 ch) in each ch-sp around, sl st to join. Fasten off.

Round 4: Join yarn D in any 2ch-sp, 3 ch (counts as 1 tr), 3 tr in same space, 4 tr in next 2ch-sp, 2 ch, *4 tr in next 2ch-sp, 4 tr in next 2ch-sp, 2 ch; rep from * 6 times, sl st to join. Fasten off.

Round 5: Join yarn E in any 2ch-sp, 4 ch (counts as 1 tr, 1 ch), 1 tr in same 2ch-sp, 1 tr in each st to next 2ch-sp, *(1 tr, 1 ch, 1 tr) in 2ch-sp, 1 tr in each st to next 2ch-sp; rep from * 6 times, sl st to join. Fasten off.

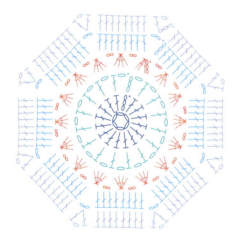

Motif 92:
Puff Flower Octagon

I've used pink puff stitches and a yellow centre to create a delicate flower at the heart of this octagon.

Yarn A
208 Yellow Gold

Yarn B
222 Tulip

Yarn C
258 Rosewood

Yarn D
524 Apricot

Yarn E
130 Old Lace

Do not turn work throughout.
Using yarn A, 6 ch, sl st to first st to form a ring.
Round 1: 1 ch (does not count as a st), 16 dc into ring, sl st to join. Fasten off.
Round 2: Join yarn B in any dc, 3 ch, 1 BegPuff, 5 ch, miss 1 dc, *(1 puff, 5 ch, miss 1 dc); rep from * 6 times, sl st to join.
Round 3: Join yarn C in any 5ch-sp, 3 ch (counts as 1 tr), 6 tr in same 5ch-sp, 7 tr in each 5ch-sp around, sl st into top of first 3 ch to join. Fasten off.
Round 4: Join yarn D in any space between sets of 7 tr, 4 ch (counts as 1 tr, 1 ch), 1 tr in same space, (1 ch, miss 1 tr, 1 tr) 3 times, 1 ch, miss 1 tr, *(1 tr, 1 ch, 1 tr) in space between sets of 7 tr, (1 ch, miss 1 tr, 1 tr) 3 times, 1 ch, miss 1 tr; rep from * 6 times, sl st to join.
Round 5: Join yarn A in any ch-sp, *(1 dc, 1 ch, 1 dc) in ch-sp, 1 dc in each ch-sp and tr to corner; rep from * 7 times, sl st to join. Fasten off.

Notes
This design uses beginning puff (BegPuff) and puff stitches. For instructions, see page 17.

Motif 93:
Chain-space Octagon

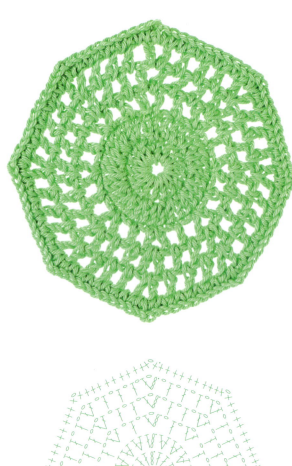

You can make this fresh motif as big as you like; just keep repeating round 4 before finishing with round 5.

Yarn A ▇
389 Apple Green

Do not turn work throughout.
Using yarn A, 4 ch, join with a sl st to 1st ch to make a ring.
Round 1: 3 ch (counts as 1 tr), 15 tr in ring, join with a sl st to top of 3 ch.
Round 2: 3 ch, 1 tr in same tr, 2 tr in each tr around, sl st to join.
Round 3: 4 ch (counts as 1 tr, 1 ch), 1 tr in same tr, 1 ch, miss next tr, 1 tr in next tr, 1 ch, miss next tr, *(1 tr, 1 ch, 1 tr) in next tr, 1 ch, miss next tr, tr in next tr, 1 ch, miss next tr; rep from * around, join with a sl st to 3rd ch of beg 4 ch.
Round 4: Sl st into corner ch-sp, (4 ch, 1 tr) in same space, (1 ch, miss next tr, 1 tr in next ch-sp) rep to corner ch-sp, *(1 tr, 1 ch, 1 tr) in corner ch-sp, (1 ch, miss next tr, 1 tr in next ch-sp) rep to corner ch-sp; rep from * 6 times, sl st to join.
Round 5: Rep round 4.
Round 6: Sl st to corner space, *(1 dc, 1 ch, 1, dc) in 1 ch corner space, 1 dc in each tr and ch-sp to next corner space; rep from * 7 times, sl st to join. Fasten off.

Motif 94:
Solid Pentagon

Pentagons don't lie flat when joined together – so they are perfect for 3D projects like a decorative ball.

Yarn A
113 Delphinium

Yarn B
222 Tulip

Yarn C
115 Hot Red

Yarn D
245 Green Yellow

Yarn E
130 Old Lace

Turn after each round.
Using yarn A, 4 ch, sl st to first st to form a ring.
Round 1: 3 ch (counts as 1 tr), 2 tr in ring, 2 ch, (3 tr, 2 ch) 4 times in ring, sl st to top of 3 ch, turn. Fasten off.
Round 2: Join yarn B in any 2ch-sp. (5 ch, 1 tr) in 2ch-sp, 3 tr, [(1 tr, 2 ch, 1 tr) in next 2ch-sp, 3 tr] 4 times, sl st to 3rd ch of starting ch, turn. Fasten off.
Round 3: Join yarn C in any corner 2ch-sp. (5 ch, 1 tr) in 2ch-sp, 5 tr, [(1 tr, 2 ch, 1 tr) in corner 2ch-sp, 5 tr] 4 times, sl st to 3rd ch of starting ch, turn. Fasten off.
Round 4: Join yarn D in any corner 2ch-sp (5 ch, 1 tr) in 2ch-sp, 7 tr, * [(1 tr, 2 ch, 1 tr) in next 2ch-sp, 7 tr] 4 times, sl st to 3rd ch of starting ch, turn. Fasten off.
Round 5: Join yarn E in any corner 2ch-sp. (5 ch, 1 tr) in 2ch-sp, 1 tr in each tr to corner space, [(1 tr, 2 ch, 1 tr) in next 2ch-sp, 1 tr in each tr to corner ch-sp] 4 times, sl st to 3rd ch of starting ch. Fasten off.

Motif 95:
Granny Pentagon

You can make a pentagon design a centrepiece of a larger project – just fit other shapes around it.

Yarn A ■
114 Shocking Pink

Yarn B ■
249 Saffron

Yarn C ■
253 Tropic

Yarn D ■
401 Dark Teal

Yarn E ■
130 Old Lace

Turn after each round.

Using yarn A, ch 6, sl st to first ch to form a ring.

Round 1: 3 ch (counts as 1 tr here and throughout), 2 tr in ring, 1 ch, (3 tr, 1 ch) 4 times in ring, join with sl st to top of 3 ch, turn. Fasten off.

Round 2: Join yarn B in any ch-sp, 3 ch, (2 tr, 1 ch, 3 tr) in same ch-sp, (3 tr, 1 ch, 3 tr) in each ch-sp, sl st to join, turn. Fasten off.

Round 3: Join yarn C in sp between 3 tr groups, 3 ch, 2 tr in sp between 3 tr groups, (3 tr, 1 ch, 3 tr) in next ch-sp, *3 tr in next sp, (3 tr, 1 ch, 3 tr) in next ch-sp; rep from * 3 times, sl st to top of 3 ch, turn. Fasten off.

Round 4: Join yarn D in sp between 3 tr groups, 3 ch, 2 tr in sp between 3 tr groups, (3 tr, 1 ch, 3 tr) in next ch-sp, *3 tr in each sp to next corner ch-sp, (3 tr, 1 ch, 3 tr) in ch-sp; rep from * 3 times, 3 tr in next sp, sl st to top of 3 ch, turn. Fasten off.

Round 5: Join yarn E in sp between 3 tr groups, 3 ch, 2 tr in same sp, 3 tr in next sp, (3 tr, 1 ch, 3 tr) in next ch-sp, *3 tr in each sp to next corner ch-sp, (3 tr, 1 ch, 3 tr) in ch-sp; rep from * 3 times, 3 tr in next sp, sl st to top of 3 ch. Fasten off.

Motif 96:
Peephole Pentagon

I love the open design of this five-pointed star – why not hang it in front of a window to get the full effect?

Yarn A
399 Lilac Mist

Yarn B
130 Old Lace

Do not turn work throughout.
Using yarn A, 6 ch, sl st to first st to form a ring.
Round 1: 3 ch (counts as 1 tr), 19 tr into ring, sl st to join.
Round 2: 3 ch, 2 tr in same tr, miss 1 tr, 1 ch, 1 tr, miss 1 tr, 1 ch, *3 tr in next tr, miss1 tr, 1 ch, 1 tr, miss 1 tr, 1 ch; rep from * 3 times, sl st to join.
Round 3: 3 ch counts as 1 tr (2 tr, 2 ch, 2 tr) in next st, 1 tr in next st, 1 ch, miss 1 ch, 1 tr in tr, 1 ch, miss 1 ch, *1 tr in next tr (2 tr, 2 ch, 2 tr) in next st, 1 tr in next st, 1 ch, miss 1 ch, 1 tr in tr, 1 ch, miss 1 ch; rep from * 3 times, sl st to join. Fasten off.
Round 4: Join yarn B in any 2ch-sp, 3 ch, (1 tr, 2 ch, 2 tr) in same 2ch-sp, 1 tr in each tr to ch-sp, 1 ch, miss 1 ch, 1 tr, 1 ch, miss 1 ch, 1 tr in each tr to corner, *(2 tr, 2 ch, 2 tr) in same 2ch-sp, 1 tr in each tr to ch-sp, 1 ch, miss 1 ch, 1 tr, 1 ch, miss 1 ch, 1 tr in each tr to corner; rep from * 3 times, sl st to join. Fasten off.
Round 5: Rep round 4 using yarn A.
Round 6: Join yarn B in any corner 2ch-sp, *(1 dc, 1 ch, 1 dc) in corner space, 1 dc in each tr and ch-sp to corner; rep from * 4 times, sl st to join. Fasten off.

Motif 97:
Pretty Flower Pentagon

A pretty yellow flower looks lovely at the centre of this colourful pentagon.

Yarn A
403 Lemonade

Yarn B
410 Rich Coral

Yarn C
398 Colonial Rose

Yarn D
508 Deep Amethyst

Yarn E
130 Old Lace

Do not turn work throughout.
Using yarn A, 6 ch, sl st to first st to form a ring.
Round 1: 1 ch (doesn't count as a stitch), 10 dc into ring, sl st to join.
Round 2: 3 ch (counts as 1 tr), 1 tr in same st, 1 ch, (2 tr, 1 ch) in each of remaining 9 dc, sl st to join. Fasten off.
Round 3: Join yarn B in any ch-sp with a dc, miss 2 tr, (2 tr, 3 ch, 2 tr) in next ch-sp, miss 2 tr, *1 dc in next ch-sp, miss 2 tr, (2 tr, 3 ch, 2 tr) in next ch-sp, miss 2 tr; rep from * 3 times, sl st into first dc to join. Fasten off.
Round 4: Join yarn C in any corner 3ch-sp, 3 ch (counts as 1 tr), (1 tr, 2 ch, 2 tr) in same 3ch-sp, 1 tr in each st to corner space, *(2 tr, 2 ch, 2 tr) in same 3ch-sp, 1 tr in each st to corner space; rep from * 3 times, sl st to join. Fasten off.
Round 5: Join yarn D in any corner 2ch-sp, *(1 dc, 2 ch, 1 dc) in corner space, 1 dc in each st to corner space; rep from * 4 times, sl st to join. Fasten off.
Round 6: Join yarn E in any corner 2ch-sp, 3 ch (counts as 1 tr), (1 tr, 2 ch, 2 tr) in same 2ch-sp, 1 tr in each st to corner space, *(2 tr, 2 ch, 2 tr) in same 2ch-sp, 1 tr in each st to corner space; rep from * 3 times, sl st to join. Fasten off.

100 Essential Crochet Motifs

Motif 98:
Puff Stitch Pentagon

Combine this with other puff-stitch motifs to make a really warm and comforting project.

Yarn A
249 Saffron

Yarn B
173 Bluebell

Yarn C
384 Powder Blue

Yarn D
164 Light Navy

Yarn E
130 Old Lace

Do not turn work throughout.
Using yarn A, 6 ch, sl st to first st to form a ring.
Round 1: (1 BegPuff, 1 ch), (1 puff, 1 ch) 9 times, sl st into top of BegPuff to join.
Round 2: Join yarn B in any ch-sp, (1 BegPuff, 3 ch, 1 puff), in same ch-sp, (1 puff, 1 ch), in next ch-sp, *(1 puff, 3 ch, 1 puff, 1 ch), in next ch-sp, (1 puff, 1 ch), in next ch-sp; rep from * 3 times, sl st to join.
Round 3: Join yarn C in any 3ch-sp, (1 BegPuff, 3 ch, 1 puff, 1 ch), (1 puff, 1 ch) in each ch-sp to corner 3ch-sp, *(1 puff, 3 ch, 1 puff, 1 ch), (1 puff, 1 ch) in each ch-sp to corner 3ch-sp; rep from * 3 times, sl st to join. Fasten off.
Round 4: Rep round 3 using yarn D.
Round 5: Join yarn E in any 3ch-sp, 3 ch (counts as 1 tr), (1 tr, 2 ch, 2 tr) in corner space, 1 tr in each ch and puff st to corner, *(2 tr, 2 ch, 2 tr) in corner space, 1 tr in each ch and puff st to corner, rep from * 3 times, sl st to join. Fasten off.

Notes
This design uses beginning puff (BegPuff) and puff stitches. For instructions, see page 17.

100 Essential Crochet Motifs

Motif 99:
Ribbed Pentagon

I love the fresh colour of this ribbed pentagon – or it would look lovely in white as a winter decoration.

Yarn A
392 Lime Juice

Do not turn work throughout.
Using yarn A, 5 ch, sl st to first st to form a ring.
Round 1: 5 ch (counts as 1 tr, 2 ch), *(3 tr, 2 ch); rep from * 3 times, 2 tr, sl st to join.
Round 2: Sl st into 2 ch corner space, 3 ch, (1 tr, 2 ch, 2 tr) tr in same 2ch-sp, work fptr round next tr, bptr round next tr, frptr round next tr, *(2 tr, 2 ch, 2 tr) in 2ch-sp, fptr round next tr, bptr round next tr, frptr round next tr; rep from * 3 times, sl st into top of 3 ch.
Round 3: Sl st into 2 ch corner space, 3 ch, (1 tr, 2 ch, 2 tr) tr in same 2ch-sp, work *fptr round next st, bptr round next st; rep from * along to corner ending with a fptr in last tr, **(2 tr, 2 ch, 2 tr) in 2ch-sp, *fptr round next st, bptr round next st; rep from * along to corner ending with a fptr in last tr; rep from ** 3 times, sl st into top of 3 ch.
Rounds 4–5: Rep round 3.

Notes
For instructions on front post treble crochet (fptr) and back post treble crochet (bptr), see pages 18 and 19.

124   100 Essential Crochet Motifs

Motif 100:
African Violet Pentagon

The final version of my African Violet motifs, again with spike treble stitches to outline the petals.

Yarn A ◼
249 Saffron

Yarn C ◼
115 Hot Red

Yarn B ◼
264 Light Coral

Yarn D ◼
247 Bluebird

Do not turn work throughout.
Using yarn A, 5 ch, sl st to first st to form a ring.
Round 1: 3 ch (counts as 1 tr), (1 tr, 1 ch), (2 tr, 1 ch) 4 times, sl st to join.
Round 2: Join yarn B in any ch-sp, 3 ch (counts as 1 tr), (1 tr, 1 ch, 2 tr) in ch-sp, (2 tr, 1 ch, 2 tr) in each ch-sp around, sl st into top of first 3 ch to join.
Round 3: Sl st into ch-sp, 3 ch (counts as 1 tr), 6 tr in same ch-sp, 7 tr in each of the ch-sps around, sl st to join.
Round 4: Join yarn C in any of the first tr in groups of 7 tr, *1 dc in each of next 7 tr, 1 Sp-tr (see Notes) in space between 2 tr groups below in round 2; rep from * around, sl st to first dc to join.
Round 5: Join yarn D in the 4th dc of any of the groups of 7 dc, 4 ch (counts as 1 tr, 1 ch), 1 tr in same tr, 1 tr in the next 7 sts, *(1 tr, 1 ch, 1 tr) in the next tr, 1 tr in the next 7 sts; rep from * 3 times, sl st to join.

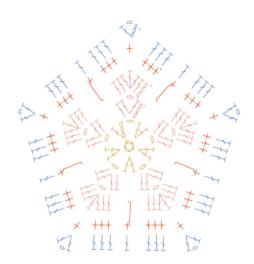

Notes
For instructions on spike treble (Sp-tr) stitches, see page 19.

100 Essential Crochet Motifs

Index

A
Abbreviations 23
African Violet
  Hexagon 80
  Octagon 115
  Pentagon 125
  Square 46
African Violet-style
  Triangle 98
Alexis Square 71
All the Blues Hexagon 84

B
Basic Techniques 10
Big Stitch Little Stitch 33
Block By Block 55
Blue Haze Octagon 116
Bobble Flower Hexagon 89
Bobbling Along Square 64

C
Carnation Square 58
Cartwheel Triangle 103
Catherine Wheel 72
Chain-space Octagon 118
Circle Granny Square 36
Circle in a Hexagon 86
Circle in a Triangle 100
Cluster Triangle Square 57

D
Daisy Daisy 34
Daisy Hexagon 78
Diamond in a Square 31

F
Flower Chain Square 67
Flower in Mesh Triangle 102

G
Granny
  Half Square 29
  Hexagon 76
  Pentagon 120
  Triangle 97
Gridlocked 65
Groovy Baby 62

H
Half Rainbow 49
Happy Flower 63
Heart Square 30
Heart Triangle 110
Hexagon 3D Flower 85
Hexagon to Triangle 101
How to Read Patterns 22

I
In a Whirl Triangle 104
In Full Bloom 66
Ivy's Triangle 107

J
Josie's Little Flower 53

K
Kaleidoscope Square 60

L
Little Granny Circle 32
Little Pearl Square 73

M
Materials and Tools 8
Matisse Hexagon 79
Mini 3D Flower 59
Mitred Flower 47
Mixed Stitch Motif 54
Moon Child 51

Moss Stitch Hexagon 87
Moss Stitch Triangle 108

N
Nordic Hexagon 88

O
Openwork Circle 95
Openwork Octagon 114
Openwork Triangle 106
Orla Square 74
Other Techniques 20

P
Peaceful Hexagon 77
Peephole Pentagon 121
Perfect Petal Triangle 109
Pretty Flower Pentagon 122
Pretty Pink Hexagon 82
Puff Flower Octagon 117
Puff Stitch Octagon 112
Puff Stitch Pentagon 123
Puff Stripe Square 37
Purple Haze 38
Purple Twist 75

R
Raised Treble Square 43
Retro Flower Motif 56
Ribbed Hexagon 90
Ribbed Pentagon 124
Ribbed Triangle 99

S
Scandi Hexagon 94
Seventies Hexagon Flower 91
She Sells Seashells on the Sea Shore 61
Sherbet Surprise 45
Sidari Square 70
Small Sunflower Square 44
Smiley Face 35
Snowflake Hexagon 93
Snowflake Square 48
Solid Granny Square 27
Solid Half-and-half Square 28
Solid Octagon 111
Solid Pentagon 119
Solid Triangle 96
Sophia Octagon 113
Spiky Circle 40
Spiral Swirl 69
Stained-glass Window Square 39
Star Hexagon 92
Starburst Hexagon 83
Starburst Motif 41
Stitches 11
Sun Square 50

T
Traditional Granny Square 26
Triangle Flower 105
Twinkle Twinkle Little Star 52

V
V-stitch Square 68

W
Wagon Wheel Hexagon 81

Acknowledgements

Creating this book has been incredible; never in my wildest dreams did I think I would be writing my third book. I would not have been able to do it without the absolutely amazing team behind me and the support of my family, especially my gorgeous boys, Harvey and Alfie, who have to put up with the extra balls of wool around the house and the occasional takeaway dinner. A special mention to my parents, who are no longer here but who were always so proud of me.

I'd like to thank the whole team at GMC for their belief in me and for allowing me to create a sourcebook that many crocheters can refer to for their projects. Thank you to Tom, who oversaw the whole process; to my tech editor on this book, Jude – it was the first time we had worked together, and she was patient, knowledgeable and kind; and to my copy editor, Alexis. Thank you also to Scheepjes for the yarn.

Finally, thank you to each and every person who has supported me along the way. Every little 'well done' or 'I love that' has given me the confidence to pursue a career I could only ever have dreamed of a few years ago.

First published 2025 by
Guild of Master Craftsman Publications Ltd, Castle Place, 166 High Street, Lewes, East Sussex, BN7 1XU, UK

Text © Cassie Ward, 2025
Copyright in the Work © GMC Publications Ltd, 2025

ISBN 978 1 78494 704 0

All rights reserved

The right of Cassie Ward to be identified as the author of this work has been asserted in accordance with the Copyright, Designs and Patents Act 1988, sections 77 and 78.

No part of this publication may be reproduced, stored in a retrieval system or transmitted in any form or by any means without the prior permission of the publisher and copyright owner.

This book is sold subject to the condition that all designs are copyright and are not for commercial reproduction without the permission of the designer and copyright owner.

While every effort has been made to obtain permission from the copyright holders for all material used in this book, the publishers will be pleased to hear from anyone who has not been appropriately acknowledged and to make the correction in future reprints.

The publishers and author can accept no legal responsibility for any consequences arising from the application of information, advice or instructions given in this publication.

A catalogue record for this book is available from the British Library.

Publisher Jonathan Bailey
Production Jim Bulley
Senior Project Editor Tom Kitch
Design Manager Robin Shields
Editor Alexis Harvey
Pattern Checker Jude Roust
Photography Andrew Perris
Crochet Charts Yasmin Megahed
Illustrations Martin Woodward
Colour origination by GMC Reprographics
Printed and bound in China

To order a book, contact:
GMC Publications Ltd
Castle Place, 166 High Street,
Lewes, East Sussex, BN7 1XU,
United Kingdom
Tel: +44 (0)1273 488005
www.gmcbooks.com